GREEK LEGENDS
FOR KIDS

GREEK LEGENDS FOR KIDS

FREE BONUS FROM HBA: EBOOK BUNDLE

Greetings!

First of all, thank you for reading our books. As fellow passionate readers of History and Mythology, we aim to create the very best books for our readers.

Now, we invite you to join our VIP list. As a welcome gift, we offer the History & Mythology Ebook Bundle below for free. Plus you can be the first to receive new books and exclusives! Remember it's 100% free to join.

Simply scan the QR code to join.

<u>Keep up to date with us on:</u>

YouTube: History Brought Alive

Facebook: History Brought Alive

<u>www.historybroughtalive.com</u>

CONTENTS

INTRODUCTION

Welcome, welcome to a magical, mystical world full of gods, goddesses, heroes, monsters and more! Prepare yourselves to enter the world of Greek mythology where we'll embark on a thrilling adventure through the lands of ancient Greece. Allow us to invite you back to those days when the gods ruled the heavens, whilst brave heroes and scary monsters battled as wise goddesses guarded the lands. For hundreds and thousands of years their tales have been retold and told countless times.

Passed through generations like the sands of time, to this day they continue to captivate, make us laugh, smile and inspire us to dream big. Young friends, you're part of the new generation that is being given the noble task of passing on these epic myths. Inside this very book are the most epic stories, heroes, gods, goddesses, monsters and more from Greek mythology.

We're sure you've heard some of these Greek myths once or twice or maybe more! Maybe you've heard of the daring feats of the mighty Hercules? Or how about the scary Gorgon, Medusa with snakes for hair? These are just some of the fascinating Greek myths that have lasted the tests of time. Prepare to meet Zeus, Athena, Hercules and many other fantastic characters. It's a journey that will take you through mystical lands where you encounter dangerous monsters and learn vital lessons along the way. Imagine cracking a code that opens the doors to a magical dimension of knowledge....well that's what learning Greek mythology is like! Truly you're about to discover so many new lessons and experiences holding timeless value.

Are you ready to embark on the journey, young adventurers? Well please fasten your seatbelts for this is about to be a joyous ride packed with magic, wonder and legendary tales that have entertained curious children just like you for a very long time. And pay attention, because there is not a second to waste!

Here is a sneak peak of what to expect inside this book....

In part 1 we'll learn about the gods & goddesses of mount olympus. You'll discover Zeus, king of all gods, Aphrodite goddess of love and many more deities.

In part 2 we'll learn about the gorgons, warriors & monsters. You'll discover the maze of the minotaur, the warrior Amazonian women and many more legends.

In part 3 we'll explore heroic quests & epic journeys. Including Hercules & his twelve labours, the fall of Icarus and many more fantastic tales.

In part 4 we'll discover myths & legends such as Pandora's box - a cautionary tale of curiosity and the Trojan war - an epic battle of heroes, gods & a wooden horse.

In part 5 we'll learn about even more gods & goddesses! Including Hades - lord of the underworld, Eros (cupid) - the mischievous god of love and many more.

In part 6 we'll learn about Greek culture & legacy. You'll discover ancient Greek heroes in the modern world, the Greek olympics - honouring the gods through sports and much more.

After we conclude our book stay tuned for you will also find some excellent activities including, mythological riddles, mythological quiz show and mythical cooking.

Greek mythology has lasted for many years because it's full of treasures of wonderful stories that will truly amaze you. Although these are more than just stories; they also contain valuable lessons about friendship, bravery and doing the right thing. Do you want to learn more and to make new friends? Of course you do! AND we're sure you want to be brave! Well you'll learn all of these important lessons, traits and much more from Greek mythology.

Now prepare your imaginations, fasten your seatbelts and join us on a magnificent and wondrous journey into the world of Greek mythology. This will be a journey that you'll never forget!

PART 1
GODS & GODDESSES OF MOUNT OLYMPUS

CHAPTER 1
ZEUS - RULER OF THE MIGHTY OLYMPIANS

Meet the powerful and intelligent Zeus, the supreme ruler of all Gods!. Actually, there is only one God king, and since he is the one in charge, he is also the most powerful god in Greek mythology. Welcome on board this journey as we investigate the magnificent and fascinating world of Zeus and his amazing exploits.

The story of Zeus begins many, many years ago in the wonderful region of ancient Greece. Born to Cronus and Rhea he faced danger right from his birth! His father, Cronus was an anxious ruler, who feared that one day his children would grow up to dethrone him. So, in his madness and greed he swallowed every child that his wife Rhea gave birth to!

Rhea knew this, but of course as a mother she deeply loved her children. Thus, she protected young Zeus by skillfully tricking Cronus to swallow a rock instead. With Cronus distracted she took the opportunity to hide Zeus in a quiet cave on the Greek island of Crete. It is here that the great, god king grew up safely on an island overflowing with majestic, wild and wonderful animals...all whilst having amazing adventures! Imagine such a place!

Young Zeus grew to be older, wiser and stronger. In due time, he went to confront his father and release his siblings from Cronus's belly. With the help of several mighty allies, he crushed Cronus and saved his siblings. Relieved the young gods and goddesses were eternally grateful and chose him as their commander. Drum roll cue...and so he became ruler of Mount Olympus!

In this heavenly realm the ancient gods and goddesses resided in majestic palaces and oversaw the Earth below. With Zeus in charge everything ran smoothly and fairly. With his strong and considerate rule, he safeguarded the world. In times of threat, he would hurl his famous thunderbolts into the sky and create thunderstorms.

The family tree of Zeus

Imagine a spiralling, massive family tree, rather like a giant puzzle. Well, this is kind of what the family tree of Zeus looked like! Poseidon the god of sea and Hades the ruler of the Underworld were his brothers. Then there was his wife, Queen Hera. Then there were his sisters Demeter and Hestia. Under them were his children....and this is where things became even more fascinating. Zeus fathered countless children with many goddesses, and even mortal women. We'll hear all about his kids later! From Athena the clever goddess of wisdom to Hermes the swift messenger, and of course Hercules the mighty half god, half human. Can you imagine a more powerful family?

Famous Zeus Myths

Zeus was at the helm of many amazing myths and stories. One of the most fascinating tales was The Titanomachy. Truly this was an epic battle of the gods versus the Titans, in fact it's one of the most famous Greek myths of all time. In this epic story the Titans attacked Zeus and his crew on Mount Olympus. However, they bit off more than they could chew! Zeus and his family fought back with vengeance to retain their place as the bosses of the universe!

Another famous myth involving Zeus was with Prometheus, a cunning Titan who stole fire from the gods and gave it to the humans. Stealing from Zeus made him furious! Zeus caught up with Prometheus and dished him out a harsh punishment, by chaining him to a rock. Here an eagle would feast on his liver every day...yikes!

Besides all this doom and gloom Zeus was also a rather amusing god. Imagine this scene. One day he disguised himself as a glamorous white bull in an attempt to seduce a beautiful princess named Europa! She was captivated by the bull's charm and climbed onto his back. Zeus galloped away and took her to the island of Crete for a magical and romantic time. Queen Hera would later find out and scold Zeus!

Young readers as our journey into the domain of Zeus the king of the gods comes to an end let us remember everything from his unusual birth and early life to his role as leader of Mount Olympus. Remember his interesting family tree, his epic tales and his legend that lives on through his most classic myths. Not only are his stories exciting, they also teach us valuable lessons about courage, leadership and that family is very, very important. Young friends anytime you hear thunder or see a flash of lightning in the sky remember that Zeus is watching over all of us with his thunderbolts!

CHAPTER 2
HERA - THE QUEEN OF MOUNT OLYMPUS

Good day young explorers! Are you ready to meet with a gorgeous and powerful queen? Well join us on an amazing voyage into the world of Hera the Queen of the Gods. Wait a minute though, let's first clear up a rumour. Being a queen wasn't all about wearing a sparkling crown and sitting on a throne. Not at all! Listen, Hera was a symbol of power, grace, and divine wisdom. So, are you ready to learn all about her stories and life lessons along the way?

Hera the daughter of Cronus and Rhea was born with beauty more mesmerising than a thousand sunsets. Zeus the king of all gods fell in love with her instantly. He was so mystified by her beauty that he just had to make her his queen. Their wedding was a spectacular event that was attended by all of the gods and goddesses of Mount Olympus. The day was magnificent, full of laughing, happiness and celebration. On this day Hera not only became the queen of the gods, she also became the goddess of marriage. From this day onwards it was her duty to safeguard the connection of love between couples.

Along with her husband Zeus she reigned over the skies. Whenever she waved her hands, the winds would blow and the clouds would gather to create thunderstorms. Although she was more than just a great natural force. Hera was also a clever and strategic thinker. She took responsibility and presided with intelligence over families and their children. With her blessings families would enjoy loving relationships.

Oh, but everyone is not perfect young readers. Even though Hera was powerful and smart, she also had a weakness. Jealousy plagued her, particularly when it came to Zeus who was infamous for his roving eye. The great god king had an unhealthy habit of falling in love with other women...and this drove Hera crazy!

One infamous story of her envy involves the mighty Hercules. Hercules was the son of Zeus' affair with a mortal woman named Alcmena. Hera learned of this and became so furious that she sent snakes to attack Hercules as a young child. But even as a boy Hercules was strong and fearless. He easily defeated the snakes and proved his destiny for greatness.

Besides her jealousy Hera did have a kind side. She frequently defended those in need and blessed the relationships of loving families. In one famous myth a mad Zeus changed a woman into a cow to shield him from Hera's wrath. With kindness Hera chose to save the woman and made her one of her priestesses.

The Marriage Goddess

Whenever couples encountered difficulties in ancient Greece they would seek advice from Hera. She guided them through all the trials and tribulations of marriage. She taught the importance of loyalty, trust and compromise in relationships. Teaching that love and respect are the pillars of lasting relationships.

As we approach the end of our wondrous journey into the realm of Hera, the mighty queen of the Gods, let's take a moment to reflect on the magical path we've travelled. From her origins to her incredible stories and her role as the guardian of marriage and families. Her marriage with Zeus, the king of the gods was nothing short of epic. Together they ruled with a majestic grace that showed us that even the most powerful beings can find strength in the bonds of love and commitment.

Hera's tale is a tapestry of wonders that has left a legendary mark on Greek mythology. When you gaze upon a colourful rainbow painted across the sky, remember that it might just be her way of showering love and wisdom upon our world. As we bid farewell to this enchanting journey, may her stories continue to live in your heart. And may you too find the strength to weather life's challenges and celebrate the joys of love, unity and understanding.

CHAPTER 3
POSEIDON - GOD OF THE MIGHTY SEAS

Ahoy there young sailors! Join us as we set sail across the deep blue, ocean waters where we will discover the magical world of Poseidon. Put on your diving masks and flippers as we dive deep into this sea god's kingdom to explore his incredible powers and the fascinating stories that have made him a legend in Greek mythology. Are you ready? Well then take a deep breath!

Imagine the vast seas with Poseidon standing upon them, tall and majestic. With his trident in hand he ruled over the waves and all of the mystical animals that lived underneath the water. But did you know that he's more than simply a sea god? He's also a master of earthquakes! Whenever the earth shakes or rumbles underneath us it is a sign to remind us of his epic power.... boom!

Hold on, and that's not all! Did you know that he created horses? It's quite funny how this all happened actually. Allow us to explain. Poseidon loved to compete. One day the goddess of wisdom Athena challenged him to design a useful present for humanity. Poseidon, not one to turn down a challenge, took his trident and smashed it into the sea. Guess what? Out popped a horse!

Meanwhile Athena planted an olive tree. Poseidon smugly smiled assuming he had won. But he wasn't the judge here...humans were given the task of choosing which was more useful: the olive tree or the horse? After thinking long and hard, they chose the olive tree. But why? Well horses are cool, but the olive tree gave them much more. It provided them with food, oil and wood. However, Poseidon's horses remain a symbol of his might and majesty.

The Mythology of Posiedon

Now we know Poseidon was a mighty God, but he did have one really bad temper! Whenever he was in a bad mood it was better to avoid him because he might unleash massive storms or huge disasters! Sailors or anyone in his way would surely perish. One such story of his infamous temper involves Odysseus. Well oopsy, because this hero made the mistake of getting Poseidon so angry that he stirred up huge storms around him! Odysseus with daring actions and smart thinking was able to navigate out and return safely to his home.

Poseidon's Marine Creatures

Poseidon ruled over the seas which overflowed with fantastic creatures that would awe any of you young explorers. He was frequently joined by his friends, the dolphins and many other fantastic creatures. Dolphins would dance with him in the waters and send his messages to passing sailors. Besides the beautiful creatures, his kingdom was also home to many dangerous monsters such as the frightening Kraken and the scary Leviathan. These fearsome sea monsters were a testament to Poseidon's epic rule!

As our journey across the seas exploring Poseidon draws to an end let us remember his powers and rule over the oceans and the earthquakes. Never forget his creation of the magnificent horses, his tails of fury and his legacy along the majesty of the seas. The next time you visit the beach and feel the salty breeze on your face, or you see the waves crashing into the sands, remember his power is all around you. Poseidon's tales will continue to captivate young sailors just like you. Allow them to inspire you to discover the wonders of the sea and the mysteries that lay beneath!

CHAPTER 4
DEMETER - GODDESS OF AGRICULTURE

Good day young farmers and nature lovers! Prepare yourselves to enter the fantastic world of Demeter, the goddess of agriculture. Join us as we unravel the mysteries of her enchanted domain. Are you ready to begin an exciting journey through the seasons, farmlands and to solve some puzzling mysteries? Well then let's go!

Born the daughter of the Titans Cronus and Rhea, Demeter was a beautiful goddess with golden hair and a heart as warm as the sun. She was the sister of Zeus and Hera; those other powerful gods and goddesses we talked about earlier. Just like them, great things surrounded her.

Demeter and The Changing Seasons

Have you ever wondered why the weather changes so much? Why is it cold in winter and hot in summer? Allow us to explain, well let's let Demeters tale do the talking! The story of the seasons begins with Demeters stunningly beautiful daughter, Persephone. One fine day she was wandering through the fields when she came across a charming stranger named Hades. He was the god of the underworld and he was captivated by her beauty. Hades really, really, really wanted to take her to the darkest realms of his kingdom. But she wasn't so sure! Would you be? Anyway, despite her protests Hades chose her as his queen.

Demeter was left feeling heartbroken and sad to lose her daughter. Her grief was so intense that the plants wilted and the ground became empty around her. It was as if the world was in sorrow with her. The gods became concerned that there would be no crops or harvest without her touch. So Zeus intervened and requested that Hades return Persephone to her mother. He said ok, but it wasn't so simple. Whilst in the underground Persephone had eaten some pomegranate seeds. This was a sneaky trick played by Hades which meant she had to spend a part of each year with him.

When she was free Persephone returned to her mother's side. During this time Demeters mood improved. Flowers bloomed and began to spring as she showered the earth with her blessings once more. With her daughter by her side, wonderful plants blossomed and prospered. But when the time came for Persephone to return to the underworld Demeter became sad. Her glum mood threw a heavy shadow over the land. The world entered the harsh days of winter. Thanks to Hades' mischief we have the seasons of spring, summer, autumn and winter.

The Eleusinian Mysteries

The Eleusinian Mysteries were special festivals for Demeter and Persephone. These special rituals took place in Eleusis; it is here that Demeter's gifts to humanity were honoured in secret ceremonies. People would travel many far from all around ancient Greece to take part in these sacred rituals. During these rituals they would be taken on a spiritual journey learning all about the secrets of life, death and the natural cycles. Those who took part in the ceremonies were thought to be blessed by Demeter. The rituals were so special that they were attended by powerful monarchs and famous philosophers such as Alexander the Great and Plato.

Demeter's presence was critical for crop prosperity and farmer well-being in ancient Greece. Farmers prayed to Demeter while they ploughed the fields, hoping for her favour and large crops to grow. She was their protector and guide, making certain that the seeds hatched and flourished into healthy plants. Ancient Greek farmers were well aware of this and expressed their appreciation and celebration of Demeter. They asked for her continuous blessings because they feared without her their crops would not grow.

Young nature lovers as we come to the end of our journey through Demeters world, let's remember her endearing relationship with her daughter Persephone. Remember the reason for the shifting seasons and their crucial role in ancient Greek agriculture. The next time you see the fields bursting with golden grains or you feel the earth underneath your feet let it remind of her magnificence. Love and appreciate the beauty of nature just like the ancient Greeks did in celebration of their beloved goddess Demeter!

CHAPTER 5
APOLLO - GOD OF THE SUN & ARTS

Well hello there and welcome to the fascinating world of Apollo, god of the sun and arts! Here we will reveal his extraordinary birth and early life on the island of Delos. Joins us to explore his fascinating duties both as the god of sun and the arts. On our journey we will make a stop to meet the mystical Oracle at Delphi. Plus, we will travel back to explore the thrilling myths of Apollo and his role in the Trojan War. Are you ready?

Apollo was born to Zeus, king of all gods and the beautiful Leto. However, their relationship was a secret (don't tell anyone) and so when Leto was pregnant with Apollo she took shelter on the island of Delos. Apollo was born on this lovely island, among golden rays of sunlight. From the beginning he was a cute and lovely child, with his golden hair and charming grin.

Apollo was gifted with powers as diverse and dazzling as the sun itself. Each day he rode his sparkling chariot across the sky providing light and warmth to the whole world. Yet his gifts went far beyond the sun. Did you know he was also a talented musician? Apollo played the lyre with grace and enchanted everyone who heard him. Oh, and he was also the god of poetry, inspiring storytellers, and their works. Wait and one more thing! Did you know he was also the god of healing? Apollo was famous for his ability to cure illness and help those in times of distress. His sacred temples, such as the one at Epidaurus, became places of recovery for the ill and sick.

The Oracle at Delphi

The mysterious Oracle at Delphi was one of the most fascinating figures related to Apollo. Ancient Greeks would visit her seeking advice on everything from personal to business decisions and much more. In a trance-like state, she would give replies that were thought to be messages from

Apollo himself. In ancient Greece, her prophecies influenced key events and shaped the path of history. To this day she is celebrated as a higher power for seeking guidance. She was kind of an ancient version of Google or ChatGPT!

Myths Featuring Apollo

The adventures and travels of Apollo are intertwined with some of Greek mythologies' most fascinating stories. Have you ever heard of the Trojan war? Well Apollo was a key figure in this epic battle where the Trojans hid in a large horse to surprise their enemies.

When Agamemnon refused to release a captive priestess, Chryseis, unleashed a fatal plague on the Greek camp. He also directed Paris's arrow to puncture the invincible Achilles' heel, resulting in the hero's demise. Such drama! Apollo's love affairs were also dramatic. He fell madly in love with Daphne but she escaped his advances by turning into a tree!

As we come to the end of our journey exploring Apollo let us remember his fascinating birth and early life on the island of Delos. A god with multiple talents and his skills. Let us also remember that he was a great healer who provided profound answers to those who sought advice from the mysterious Oracle at Delphi.

Forever Apollo's stories will motivate us to embrace our unique skills and to offer healing to the world. His relationship with the Oracle of Delphi inspires us to seek wisdom and guidance from our elders whenever we're struggling in life. Sometimes we won't know all the answers but remember there are people around you who might. Embrace your abilities, seek wisdom AND remember that you have the potential to bring your greatest gifts to the world around you!

CHAPTER 6
ARTEMIS - GODDESS OF THE HUNT & MOON

Good day young hunters and explorers! Welcome to a journey into the enchanting world of Artemis, goddess of the hunt and moon. Here we'll explore her dual nature as both a hunter and protector along with her most famous myths. But that's not all! You're in for a treat because you'll also learn about the sacred animals and symbols associated with her in Greek mythology. Indeed, these are powerful lessons to learn, so stay tuned!

Artemis was a very unique goddess, so unique that she had two parts to her personality. In one part she was a goddess of the hunt, a skilled archer with the perfect aim. She roamed in the wild hunting with a silver bow and arrows to fiercely protect all wild creatures. In particular she had a fondness for deer and bears.

Her other side was as a protector of young children and women. As the goddess of childbirth, she watched over pregnant women to ensure the children's safe delivery. In Greek mythology she is often portrayed as a crescent moon crown to signify her connection with the moon.

Artemis Famous Myths and Battles

There are many, many famous myths and battles showcasing the bravery and power of Artemis. In one famous myth she helped her brother Apollo defeat a huge, super python. This slithery, scary creature had been sent to harm her mother Leto. Thank goodness she was able to defeat it!

In another famous tale a hunter named Actaeon accidentally stumbled upon Artemis taking a bath in a sacred spring. As punishment for sneaking up and looking at her, she transformed him into a deer. He was then hunted down and killed by his own dogs...a lesson not to be sneaky!

The Sacred Animals and Symbols of Artemis

Artemis was associated with several, sacred animals reflecting her roles as the goddess of the hunt and protection. Deer, with their grace and swiftness, were very special to her. Often she was shown with a deer by her side. Whoever was caught harming a deer would be in big trouble. Other living things sacred to Artemis included bears, wild boars, hares and the cypress tree.

If you're reading or listening to this at night take a look up at the sky and look for the moon. The moon was very important in Greek mythology, and Artemis played a very important role in this connection. People believed it to be a symbol of Artemis's power and beauty. She was often referred to as "Phoebe," meaning "bright" or "radiant,". This was a sign of her connection to the luminous glow of the moon.

Artemis was the twin sister of Apollo and he was the God of the Sun, further making a strong connection between the moon and the sun. The ancient Greeks believed that the sun and the moon were heavenly chariots driven by Apollo and Artemis, lighting up the sky and guiding the world. Imagine that the next time you look up!

As we conclude our thrilling journey into the world of Artemis, the goddess of the hunt and the moon, let us be inspired by her stories. Remember her role in nature and let it remind you to be kind to nature and all of its animals. We must also be kind to all of the other people around us, and especially to protect our loved ones.

So young explorers the next time you take a walk out into nature or when you look up at the moon in the sky, remember the goddess Artemis. Let her spirit inspire you to protect and care for our beautiful world with all of its lovely creatures.

AVRERS

CHAPTER 7
ARES - THE GOD OF WAR

Good day brave young adventurers! Prepare yourselves to enter the world of the mighty god of war, Ares. This powerful god represented the fierce and brave warriors of ancient Greece. Are you ready to be inspired with courage and strength? Well let's enter the world of the great and powerful Ares!

Ares was the son of Zeus, the supreme ruler of the gods, and Hera, the majestic queen of Olympus, was a force to be reckoned with. With his powerful build and fierce presence he was a true warrior. Clad in gleaming armour and wielding his mighty spear, Ares was a symbol of strength and determination.

For the ancient Greeks, Ares represented everything related to war and conflict. His domain was battle and chaos of which he thrived in. When warriors clashed in the battlefield they believed that Ares was watching over them. Warriors and soldiers sought courage from him to fight with bravery and determination.

But there's more to Ares than just his warrior spirit! Stories from Greek mythology whisper about his secret affection for Aphrodite, the goddess of love and beauty. Despite her marriage to Hephaestus, the god of craftsmanship, Ares's heart held a hidden flame for Aphrodite, igniting dramatic tales that echoed through the ages.

Ares was the father of many mythological characters, including Phobos and Deimos, the gods of fear, and Eros, the god of love. His offspring inherited his father's powerful attributes of a god. Consequently they also had a significant influence on ancient Greece.

The Mythology of Ares

Ares can be found in many famous myths and stories from Greek mythology which showcase his strength and wisdom. In one famous myth Ares stood with the Olympian gods against some fearsome giants. Long ago the earth trembled beneath the steps of these fearsome giants who challenged the Olympian gods for the very order of the cosmos.

The mighty Ares stepped onto the battlefield and stood shoulder to shoulder with his Olympian companions, ready to confront the towering foes. As the battle raged on, the giants unleashed their devastating power upon the world. Mountains shook, rivers surged, and the very air crackled with their manic energy. But Ares was not one to be scared easily. With a roar that echoed through the heavens, he charged into battle, wielding his powerful weapons. A huge battle of epic proportions ensued! With bravery and perseverance, the Olympian gods defeated the giants. Finally, the world breathed a sigh of relief! Ares's bravery had helped them to win, his unwavering courage a siren of hope that inspired all who witnessed his heroic stand.

Perhaps another and maybe one of the most famous chapters in Ares's legendary exploits was his involvement in the Trojan War. This colossal conflict raged between the proud city of Troy and the determined forces of the Greeks. As the war's thunderous drums of battle echoed across the land, Ares took to the battlefield once again with a thunderous roar. His very presence ignited the hearts of the Trojan warriors, filling them with unwavering determination and inspiration. With his spear gleaming and armour shining, he led the charge with a ferocity that sent shockwaves through the enemy. Through the twists and turns of destiny, his presence ultimately contributed to the Trojans' success on the battlefield.

As we near the end of our journey exploring the mighty Ares let us remember his lasting impact on ancient Greek mythology. Indeed he represented the brutal side of the world that is at war. But he also inspired people with bravery and courage in times of conflict. To this day the Greeks honour him with rituals and prayers as they seek his guidance before heading into battles. These are often battles not just of fighting but battles of life and business. Even though at times he was reckless, he was also fierce and wise. He inspired many to stand up for themselves in times of adversity. So brave young warriors the next time you hear the rumble of thunder or when you are faced with challenges or bullies, remember Ares the powerful god of war. Let him inspire within you bravery and to face all of your challenges with determination. Stay strong!

CHAPTER 8
ATHENA - GODDESS OF WISDOM & WAR

Hello, hello young scholars and heroic warriors! It is here in this exciting chapter that we'll discover the fascinating world of Athena, goddess of wisdom and war. Prepare yourself to learn the truth about her unusual birth and stay tuned as we explore her special link with the city of Athens. Can you imagine someone so amazing they named a city after them? Get ready to learn all about this wise and powerful goddess!

Imagine the grand entrance of this goddess. It was unlike any other in the realms of the gods and goddesses. For she did not enter the earth in a normal way...no she sprang out from the head of her father Zeus, the king of the Gods! One cloudy day Zeus was having a horrible headache. Actually it was so terrible that he asked a strong blacksmith to split open his skull with a magical axe! The blacksmith smashed his axe into Zeus's skull. To everyone's shock out popped Athena fully grown, with a spear and shield in hand.

Athena was no ordinary goddess. From the beginning she was both intelligent and powerful demonstrating that wisdom and strength can unite in one. The citizens of ancient Athens regarded her as their protector and guardian. With her wisdom and direction, they believed their city would prosper. As we know her love of the city was so great they named it after her! To worship her, the residents built the pantheon, a mighty structure which housed a magnificent temple. Once fully built it included a famous statue of Athena holding a shield along with a small statue of Nike, the goddess of victory in her other hand.

The Athens-Poseidon Rivalry

It's well known that Poseidon the great sea god and Athena once held a friendly (and sometimes not so friendly) competition to see who would become Athens patron god or goddess. Whoever could offer the most helpful gift for the city would emerge the winner. Poseidon smashed his trident into the ground causing a powerful spring of salt water that would benefit the sailors and traders of Athens. But Athena had something better in store for the Athenians. She planted an olive tree which provided them with food, oil and wood for construction. Athena won and became their protector forever. The olive tree became a symbol of peace and wealth for Athens.

The Mythology of Athena

Athena was not just a strong warrior she was also smart and intelligent. Heroes would frequently visit her to seek guidance and courage in times of need. Her knowledge was unparalleled and unrivalled among the gods and goddesses. She became a great ally for people in search of direction and insight. When the mighty hero Odysseus faced difficulties on his return from the Trojan War, Athena was by his side guiding him.

As we come to the end of our thrilling voyage through the world of Athena let us remember her remarkable birth from the head of Zeus. With honour she guided Athens and as a wise counsellor and protected it with fever. Along with her smart intellectual powers she was also a skilled warrior. She stood tall wearing a helmet with a shield and spear ready to defend her great city of Athens. Any opponents who dared to challenge her would surely perish. Wisdom and strength can exist together as Athena exemplified.

Young warriors the next time you face a difficulty remember to seek wisdom and direction from the wise. Imagine Athena and be inspired by her just as the heroes of ancient Greece were. Let wise knowledge continue to guide you as you work to become your best selves. May you also attain greatness and become the heroes of your own epic adventures!

CHAPTER 9

HEPHAESTUS - CRAFTSMAN OF THE GODS

Good day young students. Allow us to introduce you to a god with remarkable skills that could shape the very fabric of reality. Marvellous did you say? Well, this god was certainly marvellous. His name was Hephaestus, a masterful blacksmith and a craftsman of the gods. With imagination and brilliance, he created magnificent weapons, stunning works of arts and even shaped the fabric of life itself!

Hephaestus was a truly unique figure among the Olympian gods. Born to Zeus and Hera, he was not only known for being an excellent craftsman but also for his persistence. However, he faced challenges for he was born with a disability that left him with a limp. Now he might have been disabled but he was not one to let it define him. No instead he embraced his unique talents and focused on his craft.

His creative hands breathed life into the weapons and tools that gods and heroes wielded, shaping the fates of those who inhabited this mystical world. With basic raw material hc could create magnificent works of art. One of his most famous creations was a powerful weapon for the gods. Have you ever seen the lightning bolts of Zeus? Well those were famously created by him. How about Poseidon's trident, and Artemis' silver bow? Those were also created by him, just to name a few. His skills were in demand, and his creations could be found across the heavens. He even constructed magnificent palaces for the gods, including Mount Olympus itself!

Hephaestus' Role in Mythology

Hephaestus wielded his divine talents to forge not only celestial weapons but also the very essence of Greek mythology itself. One of the most famous episodes involving Hephaestus involves his crafty ingenuity in creating some golden chains. You might think they would be jewellery, right? Well not quite! You see, to keep a god still you are going to need some strong chains. Hephaestus crafted some hefty gold chains to bind Prometheus to a rock as punishment for his stealing fire from the heavens. It was Hephaestus's skillful hand that meticulously crafted this unbreakable chain, forever binding the Titan to his rocky prison.

Another famous mythological story involving Hephaestus is the creation of Pandora, the first human woman. Zeus the king of all gods had ordered Hephaestus to shape Pandora out of clay and give her various qualities and gifts. However, she was also born with the gift of curiosity. In her possession was a forbidden box that she was told not to open. But her curiosity overcame her and she could no longer resist temptation. She opened the box, out of which spilled many troubles into the world.

Hephaestus's tales have etched a profound mark upon the canvas of ancient Greek. They teach us that with unwavering determination, creativity and hard work, even the most formidable challenges can be surmounted. His narrative is a testament to the incredible potential that is within each individual. No matter what may appear impossible, even if they come in the form of significant disabilities.

We each have unique talents and capabilities waiting to be unleashed. Maybe you wish to paint beautiful pictures, construct epic buildings or even simply to overcome challenges you encounter in life. Just as Hephaestus masterfully crafted extraordinary works, you too have the power to create remarkable achievements.

Imagine him, the next time you gaze upon a masterpiece of art or stand in awe before an amazing building. Let his story inspire the power of brilliance within you, whatever you undertake. Whether your canvas is a blank sheet, stones and rubble or the very challenges of life, remember that the power to create something extraordinary is within you.

CHAPTER 10
APHRODITE - GODDESS OF LOVE & BEAUTY

Greetings young romantics and lovers of beauty! Prepare yourselves to be fascinated by Aphrodite the goddess of love and beauty. Here in this chapter, we'll learn all about her creation, magical powers and her impact on love. Imagine a world where every moment is filled with love's gentle touch and every corner shines with beauty. That's the world where Aphrodite reigns, spreading her love far and wide.

Legend has it that Aphrodite's birth was as magical as a shimmering seashell. Once upon a time in the vast expanse of the seas, a stormy clash between the gods created waves. Among these crashing waves, something extraordinary happened. Cronus, one of the mighty Titans, decided to do a bit of spring cleaning in the sky and threw his father Uranus's severed body parts into the sea. As his watery body met the waves, a mystical froth formed, dancing on the surface like a thousand twinkling stars. From that froth emerged none other than Aphrodite! She stepped onto the shore, her radiance matching the sun's golden glow. With every step she took, flowers bloomed in her wake, painting the land with vibrant colours that had never been seen before. Her beauty was so enchanting that even the birds paused their songs just to gaze at her in awe!

Aphrodite was married to Hephaestus, the skilled blacksmith of the gods, known for crafting majestic weapons and remarkable treasures. But her heart danced to a different tune – it beat in rhythm with Ares, the daring God of War. Their love was like the clash of thunder and the sparkle of stars all at once! While Aphrodite's heart leaned towards Ares, she tried to be a loyal wife to Hephaestus. But in the world of gods, secrets are hard to keep. Gossipy breezes whispered through the heavens, and soon, everyone knew of the love that bloomed between Aphrodite and Ares.

The Power of Aphrodite

Beyond love Aphrodite was also a goddess of desire and fertility. Her powers encompassed all types of passionate feelings including those shared by friends and family. Whenever someone felt feelings of love or affection it was thought that her magical touch was at work.

All forms of beauty were thought to be gifts from Aphrodite herself. From beautiful flowers to radiant sunsets and to wondrous works of art. Furthermore, couples from all corners of the world whispered their hopes and dreams to Aphrodite. When they wanted to start families they sought her blessings. When their hearts felt tangled like a puzzle, they knew she was the one to help unravel the knots. Young lovers would gather flowers and offer them to her, asking for guidance in matters of the heart. They hoped to win the affection of those they admired, and they believed Aphrodite's magic could make even the shyest heart beat a little louder.

As we end this chapter exploring the beautiful realm of Aphrodite the goddess of love, fertility and beauty let us remember her magical creation, her powers of love, family, desire and beauty. The next time you see a flower or your heart flutters with love, remember her power is all around you. May her stories continue to inspire love and joy in your hearts. Love will come and go, and when it goes you will feel grief at its loss, but grief is a price worth paying for love. Appreciate and be grateful for all of the beauty and love all around you whilst it's here. Embrace this beautiful world around you with love.

LAND OF
HEERES

CHAPTER 11

HERMES - MESSENGER OF THE GODS & TRICKSTER

Salutations young explorers and clever thinkers! Welcome to the world of Hermes, the cunning and mysterious messenger of the gods. Join us as we learn about the myths of Hermes. Our journey will take Hermes to meet with Perseus guiding souls to the underworld to his remarkable patronage over travellers, merchants and daring thieves. Hold on tight it will be a speedy ride!

Hermes was the son of Zeus and the gorgeous Maya. Upon Mount Olympus his smart wit and charm landed him in many adventures. With extraordinary speed and amazing flexibility, he travelled quickly between the realms of gods and mortals. Thus, he was chosen as a heavenly messenger. In the twinkle of an eye with his winged sandals and helmet he could quickly travel exceedingly long distances. But watch because he was also extremely mischievous! Hermes loved to play tricks on his fellow gods and humans. Everywhere he went havoc and laughter followed him.

Hermes inventions

Do you know what a lyre is? No, it's not what you're thinking! It's actually a musical instrument. Imagine a kind of guitar, well this is what people used to play in the ancient Greek times. It was created by Herme. With his powerful imagination he took a tortoise shell and strung it with cow tendons to create this magical musical instrument. He added this along with his signature wings and sandals which allowed him to fly across the skies like a bird on a mission.

Hermes in Famous Myths

Hermes can be found in many fascinating stories and adventures. Tales that showcase his vast talents and kindness. In one such tale Hermes famously bestowed upon Perseus his wings, sandals and magical helmet of invisibility. With those precious gifts, Perseus was able to defeat the scary monster,

Medusa.

In many tales and myths Hermes played an important role in guiding souls towards the underworld. He was an expert in transporting souls to the underworld domain of Hades whilst ensuring their safe passage. Yet his influence went far beyond the worlds of gods and mortals. He was also a patron to many different groups of people. Travellers sought Hermes' protection, trusting him to keep a watchful eye on their voyages and assure safe passage through unknown lands. Merchants and traders sought direction from Hermes, who was as god of trade, bringing wealth and fortune to their enterprises. He was even known to have a soft spot for courageous criminals. He frequently bestowed them with luck and cunning, encouraging them to practise their profession skillfully. But be warned everything you do should be lawful!

Now young geniuses we are almost at the end of our journey into the world of Hermes. In a speedy journey we've explored his cunning and mysterious nature. We've learned about his creation of the lyre and the winged sandals. Plus, we've explored the thrilling myths featuring Hermes and his role in guiding souls, travellers, merchants and even daring thieves. What can we learn from all this? Firstly, Hermes teaches us the power of always learning more, to inspire us to discover joy in everyday life and to enjoy the art of mischief...but in moderation! Allow his story to inspire you to embrace your uniqueness, embark on daring adventures, and approach life with a fun spirit. Now go ahead and let your gifts shine brightly, just like the speedy messenger of the gods!

CHAPTER 12
DIONYSUS - GOD OF WINE & FESTIVITY

Welcome young explorers to the enchanted world of Dionysus, the God of wine and festivity! Join us on an exciting journey to discover his unique birth and upbringing on Mount Olympus. We welcome you to explore his roles as the god of wine, joy, lunacy and the lively! Hold steady because this will be a bumpy ride revealing extravagant festivals, lavish celebrations, intriguing myths and much more.

Dionysus was born in a very, very weird way.... Semele, the human princess, was his mother, and Zeus, king of the Gods, was his father. Once again Zeus cheated and fell completely in love with a new woman. This time it was the mortal Semele. When Zeus' wife, Hera, discovered the truth, she became very jealous and tricked Semele into looking at Zeus in his godly form. The power of Zeus was so overwhelming that Semele died as he appeared in his celestial brilliance. Zeus was helpless but he managed to save their unborn child by stitching Dionysus into his thigh until he was ready to be born. Once born, he brought Dionysus to Mount Olympus to be nurtured among the immortals.

Dionysus had a personality as colourful and varied as the colours of a rainbow! As the god of wine, he offered gifts of grapes and taught people how to make wine. He urged individuals to accept their inner impulses and to express themselves freely using wine as a symbol of joy and pleasure. Such fun it was to be around him!

Dionysus also had a darker side. Beware young readers that too much wine or alcohol might get you in trouble! He tried hard to hide his insanity and craziness. Nonetheless, he showed that there might be a balance between craziness and calmness.... even amid madness!

Ancient Greek Dionysian Festivals and Celebrations

The celebrations of Dionysus were known as Dionysia in ancient Greece. They were loud and joyous affairs! The City Dionysia in Athens, a major festival organised in his honour, was one of the most magnificent festivals. Residents would build outdoor theatres for theatrical events, including tragedies and comedies. The plays, like Dionysus' dual nature, explored human emotions and how they are often played as an inner battle between order and chaos. We have to learn to practise self-control even when we are tempted by something wrong.

The Myths of Dionysus

Dionysus embarked on many fascinating adventures with both humans and immortals. One such famous myth was his journey into the other underworld to save his mother. He journeyed deep into the dangerous underworld where Hades ruled to save his mother Semele. This demonstrated his strength and willingness to do what was right and to save his family.

Another famous myth involving him is that of King Midas. King Midas had an uncontrollable desire and this created a problem for him. Everything he touched turned to gold! Now that might seem cool, right? But what happens when you just want to eat something or to hold the hands of a loved one? Dionysus later taught him the value of simple pleasures and the importance of self-control.

Did you enjoy this journey into the exploration of Dionysus? Let us remember his dual nature as the god of joy, wine and madness! Remember the festivals that celebrate him in ancient Greece to this day. Remember the thrilling myths of his encounters with both the mortal and the immortals.

As we conclude our journey into the realm of Dionysus let us remember that we should moderate and balance in our lives. Too much excess is often a bad thing. Strive for balance young readers. Learn to appreciate the simple things in life. After all there's more to life than materialistic things or comparing yourself to someone else. Be grateful for the life you have and let the spirit of Dionysus inspire you to celebrate your loved ones. Gratitude and appreciation with moderation will lead to fulfilment.

PART 2
GORGONS, WARRIORS & MONSTERS

CHAPTER 13
THE MAZE OF THE MINOTAUR - CONQUERING THE LABYRINTH'S MONSTER

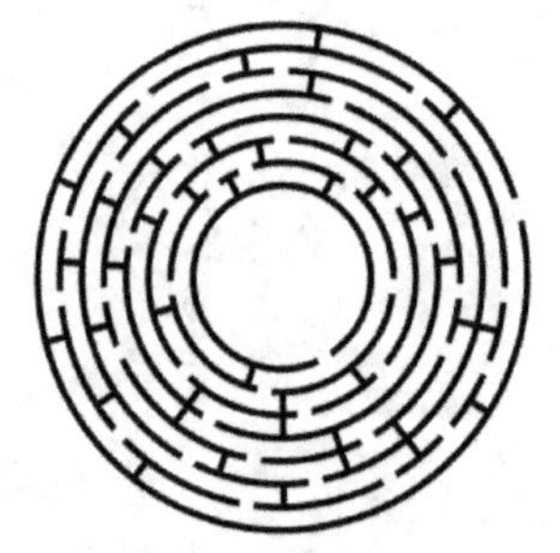

Long ago, in the mysterious times of ancient Greece, where myths and legends came to life, there was once a mighty king named Minos. He ruled over a lavish kingdom on the island of Crete. Imagine such a paradise with golden sands, blue oceans and a majestic palace upon rocks. Very nice indeed! But there was a small problem, well actually a big problem! At the centre of his paradise kingdom lay a secret that would send shivers down spines. A fearsome creature known as the Minotaur!

Now the Minotaur was not an ordinary monster. Imagine this...its head was a fierce bull whilst its body was that of a powerful man. So ugly! Unfortunately, this beast was sent as a curse by the gods to punish King Minos for his greediness. Having a monster running loose in your kingdom could be a serious issue, as you can imagine. Everywhere it went, chaos and mayhem followed, terrorising the residents of Crete.

The Maze of the Minotaur

King Minos built a massive maze beneath his palace to keep the Minotaur hidden. Deep within this labyrinth the Minotaur roamed, hungry for flesh and blood. Only the bravest (or stupidest) of souls dared to enter into the labyrinth. With its high walls, dark corridors, twists and turns it could easily confuse the smartest of heroes. But in the land of heroes, there lived a young prince named Theseus. It was he who was determined to put an end to the Minotaur's reign of terror. And as you're about to find out, he was no fool!

Theseus bravely volunteered to enter the labyrinth and face the beast. With a sword gifted from his father and a ball of thread gifted from his lover, princess Ariadne, he entered the labyrinth. At the entrance he tied one end of the thread and as he walked in deeper it unravelled behind him. This clever trick would later help him to find his way back out.

After many twists and turns, finally he reached the heart of the labyrinth where the Minotaur awaited. With his sword in hand and courage in his heart, he faced the fearsome beast. A mighty battle began and the labyrinth echoed with the clash of steel. Theseus fought with courage, using his wits and strength to conquer the beast. Finally, his sword found its mark, a weak point on the beast's neck. With one swift strike the Minotaur was defeated!

Theseus followed the thread back out through the labyrinth's twists and turns, emerging victorious. With the monster's defeat, the curse that had haunted King Minos' kingdom was lifted. The people of Crete celebrated his bravery... and for finally being freed from terror!

Theseus became a hero whose name would be forever remembered for generations to come. His story teaches us the importance of courage, determination and of facing our fears. Young adventurers, even in the darkest of mazes of life, there is always a way out. Just like Theseus found his way out, we too can overcome daunting challenges. When we stay focused, persistent and seek solutions towards our goals we too can succeed. Never give up even when it gets difficult!

So young adventurers, the next time you find yourself in a tricky situation just remember Theseus and his clever moves to emerge from the labyrinth victorious. Imagine yourself wearing his bravery like a superhero cape, armed with your own courage and clever thinking. In the labyrinth of life, every twist and turn are a chance for you to show off your own heroic spirit!

CHAPTER 14
THE AMAZONS – WARRIOR WOMEN

In the legends of Greek mythology, there once lived a group of mighty, women warriors known as the Amazons. Now these weren't your everyday heroes. Far from it! In a world where men usually ruled, the Amazons stood out like bright stars in the night sky. These fierce women held powerful positions, making choices that echoed through time. Equality wasn't just a word for them, it was a way of life.

Men and women stood side by side, sharing responsibilities and opportunities as equals. With every arrow they shot and every battle they fought, the Amazons proved that courage had no gender boundaries. They didn't just rewrite myths; they rewrote the rules of their world, showing us that true strength comes from unity and that anyone can be a hero, no matter their gender.

At a place, far at the edge of the world they lived surrounded by wild nature and never ending challenges. From a young age they were trained in the arts of combat, archery and horse riding. With unmatched abilities they rode into battle with supreme confidence instilled from their training. Their armour shined and defended against sharp attacks. And with powerful weapons in hand they defended and led their lands with determination. Yet they were more than leaders, they were also involved in many legendary tales and as we are about to discover...they feared no one!

Amazon Stories

Stories of the Amazons and their adventures can be found in many legendary Greek myths. One famous myth features Hercules on his quest to complete the twelve labours, a series of incredible challenges. During one of these labours, he crossed paths with the Amazons on a challenge to obtain the belt of their Queen, Hippolyta.

Hercules faced a tough challenge. He knew full well of the

Amazon warriors powers and respected them greatly. Only a fool would dare to battle them alone. Hercules was no fool and eventually came to an agreement where both he and the Amazon warriors were happy.

Theseus was another Greek hero who found himself up against the powerful Amazons' when he came across their fierce queen, Antiope. But here's where the story takes an unexpected turn, like a river flowing into foreign lands. Theseus and Antiope fell in love! Despite being from different worlds, their hearts connected and they fell in love. They threw down their wellness and joined forces. Love truly has the power to cross boundaries and cultures.

The tales of the Amazons, those legendary warrior women, continue to teach us powerful lessons that resonate across time and culture. Their stories are not just accounts of bravery and skill, but also hold within them deeper insights that remind us of the enduring strength of the human spirit. They weren't merely a force of fierce warriors but champions of teamwork, where different talents, backgrounds, and skills came together to create an undeniable force.

Young heroes, when you are faced with a challenge that seems impossible, think of the Amazons! In moments of doubt let the tales of these brave women who triumphed against the toughest of challenges inspire you. But remember that their victories weren't achieved alone. Just like they stood side by side and lifted each other, you too can reach higher heights through teamwork.

Regardless of where we are from or who we are, each one of us carries great potential to achieve magnificent feats. The wisdom of the Amazons teaches us to treat each and every person with fairness and value. Now venture forth with the knowledge that through unity, diversity and hard work you too can achieve greatness!

CHAPTER 15
MEDUSA - THE CURSED GORGON & HER PETRIFYING STARE

Greetings young adventures and curious minds! Have you ever heard of Medusa? Well, she was one scary monster, she had a chilling curse and some serious hair issues, snakes! In this chapter we'll learn about her origin, why she looked the way she did and the thrilling encounters she faced with brave heroes like Perseus. Finally, we'll learn about her influence in Greek arts and mythology, let's go!

Medusa was one of three Gorgon sisters who were daughters of the sea gods Phorcys and Ceto. Now the Gorgons were not like any other creatures in Greek mythology because they looked very, very different. Just imagine this...instead of beautiful hair, they had venomous snakes for hair! Oh and their eyes had a petrifying glare. Legend has it that one look into their eyes could turn anyone who dared to gaze into them into stone!

Medusa, with her fierce gaze and snake hair, was the most dreadful of the Gorgons. But why did she look like this? Well once upon a time she caught the eye of the sea god, Poseidon. It was in the temple of the goddess Athena that Poseidon and Medusa secretly met and fell in love. Athena heard about this and became incredibly angry. How dare they flirt in her temple, a place of purity! With vengeance she punished Medusa by transforming her beautiful hair into a bunch of venomous snakes! And that's not all...she also cursed her with a gaze that would turn any living creature to stone. Now as you can imagine, it's difficult to fall in love if everytime you stare at someone they freeze!

Cast out from society and cursed, Medusa wandered the desolate lands, seeking to hide from the world. Her terrifying reputation spread far and wide, reaching the ears of the heroic Perseus. With the help of Athena and other gods, he set out on a daring quest to slay the fearsome Gorgon and claim her head as a trophy.

Athena helped Perseus to find Medusa's lair where he took a polished shield as a mirror to avoid her dangerous gaze. With a swift strike of his sword he beheaded the monstrous Gorgon. His triumphant victory was a testament to bravery and resourcefulness. Perseus proved that even the most fearsome foes could be overcome with courage and quick thinking.

The Symbolism of Medusa

In Greek art and mythology, Medusa's image represents the duality of beauty and terror. The Greeks believed in the power of both positive and negative forces within the world. On one side there is beauty but another side also has danger. Life is often this way.

Medusa's petrifying gaze served as a cautionary tale, reminding mortals of the consequences of disrespecting the gods or of lying. Her image was often used as a protective talisman to scare away evil spirits and danger. Her head was often engraved on shields and armour of warriors. When faced with adversity it inspired them with courage and determination whilst setting fear in the eyes of their enemies.

As we conclude our thrilling exploration into the world of Medusa, the Gorgon with a chilling curse. Let us remember her origins, her thrilling encounters with heroes like Perseus, and her lasting symbolism in Greek mythology. Medusa's tale, or story offers us many lessons. First of all let us learn that appearances can be deceiving, and the true character of a person is on their inside. Actions will always speak louder than words. Be truthful and honest in your intentions.

Finally let the mythology of Medusa be a lesson in empathy and courage. Embrace the power of persistence and adapting like Perseus did on his quest. Remember that even in the face of the most difficult challenges, your bravery and intelligence will help you to win. May the story of Medusa inspire you to see the beauty within each soul and to conquer the challenges of your own heroic journey!

CHAPTER 16

ENCHANTING SIRENS & MYSTERIOUS CREATURES

Good day young adventurous! Are you ready to dive deep into the realms of Greek mythology? Fantastic! Get ready to uncover the mysteries of some enchanting creatures that have captivated the hearts and minds of storytellers for generations. Prepare yourself to be mesmerised by the bewitching sirens....and prepare yourself even more for other mysterious beings such as the Centaur and the Sphinx. Now let us dive into the deep waters as we dive deep into timeless lessons and fascinating moments from their captivating stories!

The Enchanting Allure of the Sirens

Far beyond the shimmering waves of the Aegean Sea up on the rocky shores, dwelt the alluring sirens. With the voices of angels and a magical beauty these enchanting creatures possessed irresistible charm. Sailors and adventurers alike were lured by their charms. With hypnotical songs they captivated even the bravest of hearts, luring ships and sailors close to their perilous shores. But one hero, named Odysseus avoided the perils.

In an epic journey home the wise hero came across the Sirens. They called out to him with hypnotic songs. Danger came closer and he had to act quickly. To protect his crew from their mesmerising songs he filled their ears with beeswax and had himself tied to the ship's mast. Odysseus very well understood their power and allure. His quick thinking and courage allowed him to safely pass their shores.

The sirens and their songs serve as a cautionary tale which teach us to be aware of the dangers of giving in to temptation. When we give into short fix, pleasure often it comes at the expense of wisdom and reason. Stay strong young explorers when you're tempted and practice self-control. Think long term. When you practise self-control and planning ahead it always pays off. In turn you will become stronger each time.

Other Mythical Creatures: The Centaurs & The Sphinx

Far beyond the shores of the sirens, lived many more extraordinary mythical creatures from Greek mythology. Brace yourself young friend for you are about to encounter the wild Centaurs and the powerful Sphinx!

The Centaurs

Half human and half horse, the Centaurs were a lively and unruly bunch, living in the untamed wild. They were famous for their wild behaviour and could often be found at the centre of chaos. One famous Centaur was the wise centaur Chiron, who was a mentor to many heroes, including Achilles and Jason.

The Sphinx

With the head of a woman, the body of a lion, and the wings of a bird, the Sphinx was a mysterious and puzzling creature. She guarded the entrance to the city of Thebes and those seeking entry first had to pass her riddles. Only one famous adventurer named Oedipus is known to have solved her riddle. As for the rest? Well one can only imagine, or lest forget!

Young explorers as we come to the end of this chapter let us explore the lessons from these mythical creatures. The Centaurs teach us about the struggle between our civilised and our wild instincts. Whilst the Sphinx challenges us to confront our knowledge and to be introspective.

Through these stories we have learned about the importance of courage, wisdom and of being self-aware. Such mythical creatures represent our own struggles and potential for greatness. Allow them to inspire you to face challenges with courage and to seek wisdom in times of doubt. As you venture out on your own heroic quests may their wisdom be your guide. May these stories inspire you with curiosity and adventure within your hearts. Until we set sail on our next voyage may these stories continue to captivate and inspire you on your own journey through life.

PART 3
HEROIC QUESTS &
EPIC JOURNEYS

HERBLLIS

CHAPTER 19
HERCULES & THE 12 LABOURS

Once upon a time in ancient Greece, there was a mighty hero named Hercules (also known as Heracles). But he was no ordinary hero; he was the strongest and mightiest of them all! Born the son of Zeus the king of all gods and Alcmena, a mortal woman. From birth he possessed incredible strength and courage. He could bend a steel bar and wrestle a lion, at the same time! But just like all heroes he faced tough challenges. His journey of greatness began with a series of incredible tasks known as the twelve labours. Are you ready to join us on a thrilling adventure to learn about his legendary feats?

The Twelve Labors Begin

The beginning of Hercules' stories starts when he tragically lost control of his actions due to a curse. In order to seek redemption, King Eurystheus tasked him with completing twelve seemingly impossible tasks. But Hercules was good friends with the impossible! So, let's join him for the twelve labours, a test of strength, wit and courage.

Labour 1: Hercules and the Mighty Nemean Lion

Hercules first task was to defeat a lion, but this was no ordinary lion. The Nemean Lion was so ferocious and powerful that it struck fear into the hearts of all who heard its name. Its coat of golden fur was so thick and strong that neither arrows or swords could pierce it. Everywhere it roamed, mayhem and terror followed.

Hercules set out on a journey through deep forests and across rivers as he followed the lion's tracks to its lair in a deep and dark cave. As he entered the cave the growls and roars of the lion echoed off the walls. But Hercules stood tall and confident, ready for whatever came his way.

The lion leapt out of the shadows and dazzled Hercules

with his fierce eyes and sharp teeth. But our brave hero was ready; he dodged the Lions' razor sharp claws and dangerous attacks. With his strength and speed he was always one step ahead.

After many hours, Hercules finally wrestled the lion onto its back. The lion roared and wriggled but Hercules held on with all of his might. He drew his sword and found a weak spot on the lion's neck. Then with one strike he slayed the fearsome beast!

With the lion slain, Hercules tore off its tough skin and used it as a coat for both victory and protection. King Eurystheus was shocked to see Hercules return with the lion's skin draped over his shoulder. Many men had been killed by the Nemean Lion, but Hercules was no ordinary man. He was a true hero who with determination and strength conquered the impossible! And it wasn't just muscles, he also used his brain to conquer the mightiest of obstacles.

Labour 2: Hercules Battles the Terrifying Lernaean Hydra

After successfully defeating the Nemean Lion, Hercules was ready for his next challenge. Only this time he would face a creature that was even more fearsome and dangerous! His target? A monstrous serpent that struck fear into the hearts of all who heard its name. Its name? The Lernaean Hydra and it lived in the murky swamps near the town of Lerna.

Now this was no ordinary snake. First of all it was big, really big. And if that's not scary enough it had nine heads which grew back every time someone tried to chop it off! Slaying such a hideous monster seemed impossible to most. But Hercules wasn't most and he was determined to prove himself once again.

With his trusty sword in hand he entered the swamps where the Hydra lurked. The air was thick with a foul smell surrounding him and the ground squished underneath his feet. Suddenly the Hydra sprang out from the water hissing and snarling. A dangerous battle began! Hercules swung his sword at the heads of the Hydra. But as soon as he cut off one head two more would sprout back in its place! It seemed like an impossible fight.

Hercules undeterred, was smart as well as strong. Something else would need to be done and so he called upon his clever nephew, Iolaus, for help. Together, they came up with a plan. When Hercules chopped off one head of the Hydra, Iolaus would burn the neck to prevent new heads from growing. Slowly and surely they chopped and burned away at the Hydra. Finally, Hercules chopped off the last head of the Hydra and returned to King Eurystheus with its remains. Once again, the King was amazed and impressed by Hercules. With teamwork, creativity and persistence Hercules had once again overcome a huge obstacle. You see strength doesn't only come from muscles but also from our adaptability to think quickly and find new ways to our goals.

Labour 3: Hercules and the Swift Ceryneian Hind

After slaying the monstrous Hydra, Hercules was given his next challenge, to capture a magnificent deer known as the Ceryneian Hind. With its golden antlers and incredible speed, this was no ordinary deer. So of course, catching it would require someone far from orignary!

The Ceryneian Hind lived in the lush forests of a distant land. With its swift legs it could outrun even the fastest of hunters. With its golden antlers it shone brightly like the sun. King Eurystheus, who had assigned Hercules this labour, believed that capturing such a rare and swift creature would be nearly impossible.

Hercules knew better and was confident in himself as always. Deep into the wilderness he ventured, marvelling at the beauty of nature as he travelled. After many days of searching he finally spotted the Ceryneian Hind grazing near a crystal-clear stream. The Hind noticed Hercules and darted away with lightning speed, disappearing into the dense woods. Capturing such a swift creature would not be easy.

Hercules chased after the Hind, racing over steep hills and under deep valleys. With a relentless pursuit he caught up with Hinds speed. As the chase continued Hercules skillfully manoeuvred the Hind into a corner. The Hind was nervous but with kind words and soothing gestures Hercules gently approached. Miraculously, it seemed to understand that he came without harm and stood still as Hercules secured a golden rope around its neck. With grace Hercules led it back to King Eurystheus who was amazed at his ability to capture such an elusive creature without causing it harm. Respectfully he realised that Hercules was not only strong, but was also kind and clever.

Labour 4: Hercules and the Wild Erymanthian Boar

After capturing the Ceryneian Hind Hercules was faced with yet another challenge. Another capture! This time it was the challenge of capturing the Erymanthian Boar, a wild and mighty beast that caused chaos wherever it roamed.

Hercules ventured deep into the lush forests on the slopes of Mount Erymanthus where the bore resided. After many days of searching Hercules finally saw the wild boar tearing through the forest with sharp tusks and powerful hooves. Scrambling up a snowy slope he chased the beast where slippery grounds made it difficult for the boar to maintain its balance. As the beast slipped down the ice, Hercules skillfully trapped it in a net.

The wild boar thrashed around in the net but Hercules held on with all of his might. With the boar thrashing in his hand he journeyed back through fierce storms and across treacherous cliffs. Finally, he arrived back to present the Erymanthian Boar to a shocked King Eurystheus. The king congratulated Hercules for his strength to capture this fearsome beast and his resourcefulness to return with it. In a dangerous and impossible situation he had once again emerged triumphant

Labour 5: Hercules and the Augean Stables

After capturing the Erymanthian Boar, Hercules faced a new task assigned by King Eurystheus. After all the capturing it was time for something else, to clean the Augean Stables in a single day. However, these were not ordinary stables. Home to a vast number of cattle and they had not been cleaned for many years, creating a colossal mess!

Our hero Hercules was not lazy and did not procrastinate. He approached the Augean Stables with a determined spirit, even though he could smell the stench from miles away. The size of the stables was overwhelming, but Hercules was not one to back down from any challenge. With his powerful muscles and sharp mind, he devised a clever strategy to clean the stables in a record time. With bare hands he dug deep tunnels to redirect nearby rivers to flow through the stables and wash away the filth. The waters crashed in and washed away years of filth. Once again, the air was filled with freshness, ahh.

King Eurystheus was astounded when he learned of how quickly Hercules had completed the seemingly impossible task. Finally, the Augean Stables were clean and free from the mess that had plagued them for so long. Hercules used his intelligence and creativity to find an innovative solution to the task at hand. With hard work we can achieve a goal. But sometimes we have to think creatively to adapt. Instead of avoiding enormous tasks, roll up your sleeves and get to work!

Labour 6: Hercules and the Stymphalian Birds

For his sixth labour Hercules was faced with a winged menace, the Stymphalian Birds. These were gigantic birds with sharp beaks and feathers that were tough as metal. Those unfortunate souls nearby lived in fear as the nasty birds caused havoc and terror.

Hercules set out to end their reign of terror. As he arrived at the marshes where they lived he noticed that they were swift and elusive. So instead of rushing in, he thought carefully about a plan to defeat the birds on their own terrain. You see, oftentimes instead of rushing in with overconfidence we need to take a step back and think of a more creative solution.

Hercules took a pair of bronze clappers gifted from the goddess Athena to scare the birds out of their hiding spots. With a loud noise from the clappers, he scared the birds into flight. As the birds soared into the sky, Hercules aimed his arrows. With a sharp aim he shot down the menacing birds one by one. Finally, peace was returned back to the land.

Labour 7: Hercules and the Cretan Bull

For his seventh labour, Hercules faced a fearsome beast known as the Cretan Bull. This was an enormous bull with powerful muscles and sharp horns that could pierce through anything. Destruction and devastation lay in its tracks. Farmers, where the bull roamed were fed up and so they called upon Hercules to save them.

Hercules set out for Crete where he found the bull wreaking havoc, but he was not one to be intimidated. As the bull charged at him he grabbed onto its powerful horns and with his incredible strength wrestled it to the ground. With his bare hands he submitted the mighty beast. After capturing the bull, he was faced with the challenge of getting it back to King Eurystheus. With big muscles like a powerlifter, the mighty Hercules simply lifted the bull onto his shoulders and carried it all the way back to the king!

With determination and resourcefulness Hercules was again successful. Even though he was strong, he was also compassionate. He didn't use his advantages to bully or to harm others. Instead, he used it to protect and to help those in need. Remember that our talents and abilities should be used to make the world a better place.

Labour 8: Hercules and the Mares of Diomedes.

Onto the next adventure! For his eighth labour Hercules faced wild and dangerous creatures, the Mares of Diomedes. These were a group of fierce and hungry horses that loved to feast on humans! A cruel King named Diomedes was their owner and he was happy to let them feed on captured travellers. Meanwhile villagers living nearby were terrified of the monstrous creatures and begged Hercules for help.

Our hero Hercules set out on a journey to capture the horses and bring them to King Eurystheus. Protected by his lion's skin and with his trusty club in hand he arrived at the stables where the horses lived. As he approached he saw their red eyes gleaming with hunger. Hercules took a step back and waited until night time. The horses would be sleeping then. Under the cover of darkness he sneaked into the stables. Using his big muscular strength he submitted and tied up the horses.

But it didn't end here....King Diomedes learned that someone was daring enough to steal his prized horses. Furiously he gathered an army and attacked Hercules. A dangerous battle ensued. But Hercules was no pushover! With his mighty club in hand and quick thinking he defeated the king's soldiers. He led the tamed horses back to King Eurystheus, who congratulated his bravery and determination. Once again he proved his ability to conquer even the most ferocious beasts. And just like Hercules, you too have the power to stand up against challenges and make a positive difference.

Labour 9: Hercules and the Belt of Hippolyta

Hercules continued his daring adventures with each labour testing his courage and strength. The ninth labour was no exception, for on this adventure his task was to obtain the magical belt of Hippolyta!

Hippolyta was the queen of the Amazons, a tribe of warrior women. She possessed a beautiful and powerful belt. Legend has it that this belt would give strength and protection to its wearer. King Eurystheus sent Hercules on a mission to capture this remarkable belt.

Hercules arrived and asked Hippolyta to give him the belt peacefully. Why not she thought? After all, she was impressed by Hercules's bravery and agreed to give him the belt as a gift. However, the jealous goddess Hera, who always caused trouble for Hercules, decided to meddle in their encounter. She stirred up and spread rumours that Hercules was planning to capture Hippolyta, then steal the belt. Confused and misled, her warriors clashed with Hercules in battle. Hercules tried to explain but in the end he had to forcefully capture the belt. With the belt in his hand he left the land of the Amazons saddened by what had occurred.

Sometimes young adventures our messages and intentions can be misunderstood. We must listen, clarify and trust each other. Just like Hercules, try to always find peaceful solutions to our problems. Keep a clear head and never allow rumours to cloud your judgement.

Labour 10: Hercules and the Cattle of Geryon

On his tenth labour Hercules would have his courage and determination tested once again. This time he was tasked with capturing the magnificent Cattle of Geryon. Now Geryon was a farmer but he was not an ordinary farmer...he was a giant with three heads and six arms!

Geryon owned cattle that were dazzling with red hides and were famous for their strength and speed. King Eurystheus, commanded Hercules to bring back these extraordinary cattle. Hercules travelled across deserts, mountains, and vast lands on his journey to the far western reaches of the world where the cattle grazed. As he arrived at the dwelling of Geryon he was faced with a fierce two-headed guard dog named Orthrus. With his powerful club, Hercules smashed Orthrus and moved forward to face the next part of his quest.

Finally, our brave hero encountered the giant Geryon, but he was not happy to see intruders on his land. Hercules wrestled with Geryon's multiple arms. Once again, his strength was the strongest. He emerged victorious and went on to capture the cattle of Geryon. Hercules created a massive bronze vessel to carry the cattle across the seas back to King Eurystheus.

However, the journey back was not a smooth one for along the way Hercules was met with the god Helios. Frustrated by the blazing heat Hercules shot an arrow at the sun. Helios was impressed and gifted him with a magical golden cup allowing him to travel over the sea with ease. Eventually Hercules reached King Eurystheus and presented him the Cattle of Geryon. With determination, creativity, and a willingness to face challenges head-on, Hercules completed his tenth labour.

Labour 11: Hercules and the Apples of the Hesperides

For his eleventh labour Hercules faced an incredible challenge. His mission? To retrieve some golden apples which were guarded by the Hesperides, three skilled and powerful women who lived in a magical garden at the edge of the world.

The golden apples were said to be a gift of immortality to anyone who ate them. Of course, everyone wanted a bite! Including King Eurystheus who sent Hercules to bring back these special apples as part of his ongoing trials. And so he set out on his journey to the Garden of the Hesperides.

Once he reached the garden, Hercules was faced with a fierce dragon named Ladon. Its many heads and sharp teeth made it a dangerous opponent. But Hercules was not scared and with bravery he slayed the fierce dragon. However, he was soon faced with a new challenge. For now, he was met with the Hesperides, who were the daughters of the titan Atlas. With their magical skills they created powerful illusions and tricks to confuse and distract Hercules.

Hercules offered their father, Atlas, a deal. He would temporarily hold up the sky (which was Atlas's punishment) in exchange for Atlas retrieving the golden apples for him. Atlas agreed, and as Hercules held up the sky, he went to the tree and retrieved the apples. However, Atlas tried to trick Hercules to continue to hold up the sky, but Hercules was no fool. Hold this a minute, he said to Atlas as he escaped with the golden apples.

Hercules triumphantly returned to King Eurystheus with the golden apples in hand. The golden apples became a symbol of Hercules's ability to find innovative solutions and use strength to achieve goals. As you face your own adventures, Hercules's journey to retrieve the golden apples inspires you to think outside the box, believe in your abilities, and never give up.

Labour 12: Hercules and the Capture of Cerberus

Are you ready to embark on one last thrilling adventure? Join Hercules on his twelfth and final labour where he was faced with capturing the Cerberus. Again a capture mission! This time to catch a horrible dog with three heads, sharp teeth and a tail made of serpents!

Cerberus lurked in the Underworld which was a tricky place to find. Hercules asked for help and was guided by the goddess Athena. Once he reached the gates of the Underworld he was met with Cerberus. The dog barked and growled at him with eyes that glowed with fire. Hercules wrestled with Cerberus, its three heads snarled and snapped, but he held on tightly. Slowly, the horrible dog faded as he was brought under Hercules's control.

With the dog in hand, Hercules journeyed back to the world above and presented it to King Eurystheus. The king was both amazed (and frightened) to see the dog with its three heads. Once again Hercules had proven himself as the greatest hero of all time!

Hercules' Twelve Labors proved his amazing abilities, strength and determination. Time and time again he proved that with a strong heart and fast thinking, even the most difficult challenges could be overcome. For when faced with seemingly impossible challenges, he never gave up. Instead, he looked at it from a different angle or thought creatively of solutions to emerge victorious. Not only with his strong muscles but also using his brain and brilliance. Hercules' reminds us that hard work, persistence and creativity will help you to conquer many obstacles in your life. With the right mindset and the belief in yourself, you too can emerge victorious in your own challenges!

CHAPTER 20
THE FALL OF ICARUS - A LESSON IN CONSEQUENCES

Once upon a time in the world of ancient Greek mythology there lived a daring and adventurous young boy named Icarus. Together with his father Daedalus, he lived on the island of Crete. Daedalus was a brilliant inventor, world famous for his amazing creations and brilliant inventions. But guess what? He was hiding a huge secret! What do you suppose it might be? Keep reading to learn more about this amazing invention that was so thrilling it was like putting a rainbow in a jar.

One rainy day, Daedalus and Icarus found themselves trapped on an island by a wicked king who refused them to leave. The king knew very well that Daedalus skills were just too valuable to lose. Daedalus on the other hand could not wait to escape back home with his son. And so, he went to work on a fabulous invention, creating a pair of wings to escape. Crafted with the threads of courage and dreams of home, these wings were given to young Icarus.

Daedalus gifted Icarus the glorious new wings. He showed his son how to wear them and how to soar gracefully in the skies. However, they came with a serious disclaimer. Now listen closely because such a warning should not be taken lightly! Daedalus cautioned his son to be careful, don't fly too low or the sea would clog his wings. Additionally, he warned him not to fly too high because the sun's heat would melt them.

Icarus jumped into the air and with the magnificent wings he took flight, his heart racing with excitement. As he soared into the skies, he felt amazing and couldn't contain his joy. Higher and higher he flew, feeling like he was invincible. But as he flew higher, he became careless and ignored his father's advice. Soon he came very close to the warm sun. Feeling its enticing warmth, he thought if he could just touch the sun, it might make him even more powerful. So, ignoring the voice of reason in his head, he flew closer to the hot sun.

Suddenly disaster struck! The wax that held his wings together started to melt as he got closer to the sun. Icarus felt his wings collapsing, and he fell swiftly towards the sea below. Desperately he flapped his wings as the winds whipped around him, but it was too late. He crashed into the sea, falling at a place that was named the Icarian Sea in his memory.

Lessons from a cautionary tale

Now what can we learn from this cautionary tale of Icarus? First of all, we must always be cautious with pride and arrogance. You see Icarus was carried away by his overconfidence and excitement. This created an attitude of arrogance which eventually got the better of him and turned things sour. In his ignorance he didn't listen to his father's warnings. He thought he could rise above the laws of nature. Such foolish actions eventually led to his downfall.

Young explorers, whenever you see the birds flying across the sky or you feel the warmth of the sun, remember the story of Icarus. Be careful to stay humble even when the dazzling lights of praise flash upon you. Understand that often when our dreams come to life, it can be all too easy to fall from grace. Just like Icarus dreamed to fly yet quickly crashed into the sea. Stay humble with an open mind and listen to those wise people who care about you. Dream big, but stay humble and who knows, you might discover your own wings of wisdom!

CHAPTER 21

ODYSSEUS' EPIC ODYSSEY - THE CLEVER TRAVELS OF A HERO

Once upon a time in the ancient world of Greek mythology there lived a hero named Odysseus. But he was unlike many of the other heroes you've heard about so far. So far we've heard tales of the strong and mighty. But, Odysseus was famous for his intelligence, quick thinking, and creative solutions even in the trickiest of challenges. Let's visit him to see how sometimes a strong brain is more useful than titan size muscles!

Born in the city of Ithaca, Odysseus fought bravely in the Trojan War. After ten long years this epic battle finally came to an end. The Greeks emerged victorious and Odysseus set sail for his homeland ready to reunite with his family. However, his journey back would not be a smooth one. For he sailed across a massive and chaotic sea where he was met with many, many challenges. In Greek mythology his journey became known as "The Odyssey". It is a legendary tale of bravery, perseverance and creativity. Now, let's dive into the adventure!

The Odyssey

Picture Odysseus, a captain with a heart full of courage as he sets sail back to his beloved Ithaca. But before he even set sail, the waves themselves held a grudge! Poseidon, the mighty sea god, was furious at Odysseus for blinding his son, Polyphemus, during the Trojan War. So, he stirred up storms that wreaked havoc on their ship, pushing them toward the clutches of the one-eyed giant, Polyphemus, also known as a Cyclops.

Fear not, for wit and bravery were abundant in Odysseus' and his loyal crewmates! In the belly of the beast, they hatched a clever scheme. They presented themselves as "Nobody" to the Cyclops. And when Polyphemus cried for help, "Nobody" was to blame! The cunning plan worked, and with eyelids heavy from laughter, they managed to escape the giant's grasp.

But the adventures didn't stop there! Every island in their pathway seemed to hold a new challenge and presented a new twist to their story. As they passed one island the sailors met the Lotus Eaters. They tricked the sailors with fruits that made them forget their homes, like a temporary spell of forgetfulness. If that wasn't enough on another island they met the Sirens. Their mesmerising melodies lured sailors toward danger, crashing close to the rocks. However, with sharp wits they steered away from danger.

Further on they sailed, only to be met with Circe, a sorceress with many sneaky tricks rolled up her sleeves. She tried to turn Odysseus' crew into animals! But once again with his sharp mind, he outsmarted her spells, steering his ship away from her tricks. Next Calypso, a captivating beauty, offered him the allure of eternal life. Only this came at the price of forever leaving his homeland behind. Not such a great deal!

Even in the tight grip of a sea monster called Scylla and a swirling whirlpool, Odysseus kept his crew's courage afloat. He used his wit to navigate through narrow straits, just like threading a needle through a stormy sea. With each challenge, he stood as a beacon of bravery and cleverness. He played the hero's part, unravelling problems with his quick thinking and persistence. Throughout his adventure, Odysseus used creative solutions, bravery and determination to rescue his crew.

Finally, Odysseus returned to Ithaca. But even there, his journey was far from over. For it was here that he had to prove his identity to his own wife, Penelope and scare off the men who tried to marry her. He called for help from his son

Telemachus and the goddess Athena. Together with their help, Odysseus once again emerged victorious.

So, young adventurers, what can we learn from this? Understand that the key to success is not just being stronger but being smarter. Beyond having muscles like a titan, it's also about flexing your brainpower! Odysseus faced monsters, tricky challenges, and even heartache. But with intelligence, resourcefulness and persistence he always succeeded.

As you sail through your own adventures, remember his lessons. For you also don't need a sharp sword or big muscles to conquer challenges. A sharp mind with a brave heart is often more useful. Just like Odysseus, navigate the seas of life with cleverness and courage. In doing so you'll find that even the toughest challenges can be conquered with a clever mind and a sprinkle of bravery.

CHAPTER 22

ECHO & NARCISSUS - A LOVE STORY OF ECHOING HEARTS

Once upon a time in the magical world of Greek mythology, there was a young beautiful woman named Echo. She was famous for her beautiful singing voice which could mimic any sound that she heard. Echo loved to wander through the deep forests singing and imitating the calls of the birds and animals.

One day she came across the king of all gods Zeus. He was a flirtatious God but he was married to Hera. Anyway, he was the mighty king of all gods, so what! And so he flirted with Echo. Hera learned of their betrayal and as punishment she cursed Echo by taking away her ability to speak her own words. From then on, she could only repeat the last words that were spoken to her.

Echo still wandered through the woods day after day. One day she came across a handsome youth named Narcissus. He was famous far and wide for his handsome looks, but he had a flaw. Narcissus was so obsessed with himself, he cared for no one or nothing else but himself. Thus, he reflected the affections of all who loved him.

Narcissus was famous for breaking hearts with indifference. Many of the most beautiful women fell in love hopelessly with him. One of those was Echo. She longed to express her feelings to Narcissus. But she was only able to repeat words. Day after day she followed him through the woods hoping he would notice her.

One day, as Narcissus was separated from his companions, he called out, "Who's here?" Echo, as she always did, repeated his words, "Who's here?" Confused, Narcissus looked around and saw no one. He called out again, "Come!" And once again, Echo echoed his words, "Come!" But still, he saw no one.

Now he was even more confused and also a little annoyed,

he called out, "Let's meet!" Echo echoed his words, "Let's meet!" Unable to understand that the voice was his own repeating, Narcissus grew frustrated and yelled, "Leave me alone!" And yet again, Echo echoed his words, "Leave me alone!"

Feeling frustrated and embarrassed, Narcissus ignored the voice and continued his journey. However, he didn't realise that the voice belonged to the young girl who had fallen in love with him. Echo's heart ached as she watched him walk away, knowing that he would never truly see her or hear her feelings.

Narcissus' self-centred attitude eventually led to his own downfall. As he looked at his own reflection in a pool of water he fell in love with what he saw. Unable to tear himself away, he wasted away as he longed for his own reflection until he transformed into a beautiful flower – the narcissus flower.

The story of Echo and Narcissus represents love and self obsession. The voice of Echo lives on as a natural phenomenon of an echo or a reminder of a love that was never truly heard. Whilst the narcissus flower blooms as a reminder of the dangers of excessive self love and vanity.

Let their tragic love story remind us of how important empathy, understanding and valuing the feelings of others really are. For love is not a selfish act, it is a shared feeling. And remember that true beauty is not just in someone's physical looks but it also in their hearts and actions.

CHAPTER 23
THE DARK RIVERS OF THE UNDERWORLD

Did you know that a second world once existed deep beneath the surface? Would you be interested in learning the mysteries of it? In ancient Greek mythology, the underworld was the name for this mysterious place. After leaving the world of the living, the spirits of the dead had to travel here. However, to reach there, one first had to navigate the vast Underworld rivers guided by a chilling character named Charon.

The underworld was surrounded by dark rivers flowing through caverns and tunnels. But these rivers were not like the ones we see on Earth; they were magical and held great powers. One of the most important rivers was the River Styx. According to legend it was the boundary between the word of the living and the dead. One had to cross this river on their journey to the afterlife. But they needed to please someone first.

Charon, The Ferryman of the Underworld

Meet Charon, a fascinating and mysterious character. It was he who played a very important role in journeying souls to the underworld. Imagine an old hooded man with a long grey beard. Each and every day the old man would ferry the souls of the deceased across the River Styx to the underworld.

His boat was a magical ship that could transport souls from this world to the afterlife. But he wouldn't just take anyone across that river. Deceased souls had to pay him with a special coin which would be traditionally placed under their tongues before they were buried. This coin, known as an obol, was accepted as payment to guarantee a secure journey to the Underworld.

And for those who couldn't afford the payment. Well, their fate was to wander the shores of the River Styx for one hundred years unable to cross nor find any rest. This is why it was so important for the ancient Greeks to always place coins on the eyes and mouths of their deceased. Because they wanted to ensure that their trip to the end of the world was secure. Be sure to save some money too!

Dear young friends remember, the River Styx isn't just a mythological river! It is also a reminder of the challenges and choices we will all face. Just like Charon guided souls, you too will also have to guide your life through many challenges. But if you focus on being prepared and consider the consequences of your choices then you will make better decisions.

In this tale, those who didn't pay Charon were stuck on the shore of the River Styx, unable to cross. It's a reminder that when we're not prepared, we might miss out on opportunities or face setbacks. So, young adventurers, take this lesson to heart. Make responsible choices and be prepared for whatever life brings your way. So as you journey through your own rivers of life keep these lessons in mind. Prepare, make smart choices and steer your boat with confidence!

CHAPTER 24
JASON & HIS QUEST FOR THE GOLDEN FLEECE

Good day young adventurers and brave explorers! Welcome to an epic journey where we will join the mighty Jason and his brave crew, the Argonauts on their quest for the mysterious Golden Fleece. Are you ready for a journey across the seas with this team of smart and strong adventurers? Stay tuned to learn all about the great challenges and adventures they faced on their thrilling search for the Golden Fleece. Truly, this is one of the most famous adventures in Greek mythology!

We begin the story with Jason, a brave hero who set out to claim his rightful place as the king of Iolcus. He stood at a crossroads of life with a huge decision before him. In order to claim his throne, he would first need to fetch the Golden Fleece. Whoever claimed the mysterious and powerful fleece would be worthy of a crown. However, the quest for the elusive fleece would test his strength, intelligence and heart.

Jason and the Argonauts

Jason gathered together a fearless band of heroes known as the Argonauts. Together they boarded a magnificent boat built by skillful craftsmen and followed the guidance of the goddess Athena herself. Far off to the distant land of Colchis they set sail on their great adventure. It is here that the elusive Golden Fleece was guarded by both mortal and supernatural challenges.

But wait! Because before we get there we must sail across dangerous waters. On these very waters the courageous team battled ferocious monsters and faced the wrath of the gods. In one challenge they came close to clashing against the rocks as huge boulders smashed down the cliffs! But with the guidance of the goddess Athena, Jason and his crew safely manoeuvred through the perils.

When they reached the land of Colchis, Jason faced his

most challenging task, he had to convince King Aeetes to give him the Golden Fleece. Jason stood before the mighty king. With determination shining in his eyes, he pleaded with the king to grant him the Golden Fleece. But the old king was not about to hand over his most treasured possession so easily. For his heart was as tough as armour, and he refused to part with his cherished prize!

It seemed like all hope was lost, that is until a glimmering figure stepped onto the stage of destiny. Who might this figure be, you ask? None other than Medea, the daughter of King Aeetes. She was no ordinary princess. More than that she was also a sorceress with a heart full of kindness and.... a spark of love for our hero, Jason. Ah, young love! Her heart was swayed by the bravery of our daring hero and she decided to help him.

With a touch of magic, Medea put the fearsome dragon that guarded the Golden Fleece into a sleep so deep that even his snoring would rival a symphony! With the dragon snuggled up in dreamland, Jason seized the moment. With silent steps and a heart pounding, he tiptoed past the sleeping dragon and claimed the Golden Fleece for his own.

The Power of Teamwork

The story of Jason and the Argonauts teaches us that courage and teamwork are powerful forces in life. Imagine you're playing a game with your friends, and everyone brings their own special skills to the table. One friend's super good at solving puzzles, another's amazing at telling funny jokes, and yet another is the fastest runner you've ever seen. When all these talents come together, it's like a magical recipe for success, just like it was for Jason and his Argonaut friends.

So, young readers, remember this epic story. It's not just about a fancy fleece, really it's about the incredible power of true friendship. Just like how Jason and the Argonauts had each other's backs, you too can achieve amazing things when you have friends who believe in you. Team up with friends who cheer for you, support you and help you reach for the stars. Who knows, you might discover your very own Golden Fleece!

CHAPTER 25

ORPHEUS THE MUSICIAN - A TRAGIC JOURNEY INTO THE UNDERWORLD

Hello there young learners. Would you like to hear about a famous musician? In this chapter we're about to learn about Orpheus, an extraordinary musician with an enchanted instrument. Here we'll embark on a captivating journey to discover his exceptional talents and the magic of his instrument. Our journey will also explore the tragic and touching tale of Orpheus and his lover Eurydice as they fell into the depths of the underworld. Finally, our journey will conclude the legacy of his melodies in Ancient Greek culture.

Orpheus was born a talented musician. From a young age he showed amazing musical talents that enchanted anyone who ever listened. With a lyre in hand (a kind of stringed instrument) he could create magical melodies that stirred the hearts of gods and mortals alike. With a gentle strum he could bring tears of joy and with powerful chords he could ignite the deepest of emotions. Legend has it that even wild beasts and trees would sway to the rhythm of his music!

Orpheus & Eurydice, A Tale of Tragic Romance

Once upon a time Orpheus fell in love with Eurydice, a beautiful young woman. She was mesmerised by the melodies Orpheus played on his lyre. But tragically, she was bitten by a venomous snake and was taken far too soon from the world of the living. Orpheus could not bear to live without his beloved. And so he set out on a daring journey to the realm of the dead, the Underworld and bring her back to the world of the living.

With his enchanting music he charmed the moody, underworld god Hades and his queen, Perspone. Mesmerised and moved by his songs they allowed him to take Eurydice back to the world above. Only on one condition... he must not look back until they had reached the world of the living. In one moment of doubt he turned around to ensure Eurydice was still with him. This mistake cost him dearly and he lost her forever. Eurydice vanished back into the shadows of the Underworld, leaving Orpheus heartbroken and alone.

The Legacy of Orpheus

Orpheus's music had a magical impact on anyone who listened. They felt emotions and were transcended beyond the boundaries of time and space. He was also a gifted poet and storyteller, using his lyrical verses to share emotional and captivating tales. His creative gifts had the power to heal hearts, inspire courage and express deep emotions of the human soul. His melodies continue to resonate throughout ancient Greek culture and beyond. To this day his legacy lives on in the hearts of those who appreciate the power of music and storytelling. Meanwhile his story has become a symbol of undying love and the consequences of recklessness.

As we near the end of our journey into the life of Orpheus, the extraordinary musician and his heart wrenching journey into the underworld. Let us remember his extraordinary talents and praise the melodies he played. There are lessons from the touching tale of Orpheus and Eurydice. It reminds us to cherish every moment with our loved ones and to never take love for granted. Time can slip away just like notes from a lyre. Like Orpheus's timeless melodies, may your own creativity and love resonate in the hearts of others.

CHAPTER 26
THE MUSES - GIFTS OF CREATIVITY & INSPIRATION

Long ago in the magical realm of ancient Greece, lived nine extraordinary beings. Together they were known as the Muses. Art, science and creativity were just a few of the wonderful things inspired by them. Each Muse had their own special talents and together they covered a wide range of fascinating subjects. Could you imagine having nine extra, magical friends to spark your imagination, teach you, or to inspire your creativity. Wouldn't that be wonderful? Well, that's what The Muses are here for. Now without further ado, let's share their gifts with you!

Calliope, The Muse of Poetry

Meet Calliope, the wisest and eldest Muse. Imagine her as the storyteller of ancient Greece, inspiring poets to write epic tales. You know, the kind that makes your imagination take flight like Pegasus! She's the reason words dance on the pages, creating magic that tickles your soul.

Clio, The Muse of History

Step into the realm of Clio, the Muse of history. She's a gateway to the past, helping historians scribble down important moments so they're never forgotten. Imagine her with a magical pen, making sure that the stories of brave heroes and legends are passed on.

Erato, The Muse of Love Poetry

Erato is the Muse of love poetry and she's like a mini Cupid spreading love through words. She whispers sweet verses into the ears of poets, making their hearts sing with love. When you read beautiful, romantic poems, you can be sure that she had something to do with them.

Euterpe, The Muse of Music

Euterpe is all about music. She's the maestro of melodies, guiding musicians to create songs that make toes tap and hearts hum. When you listen to a catchy tune that makes you want to dance, think of her leading the symphony of sounds.

Melpomene, The Muse of Tragedy

If you're in the mood for some drama, Melpomene is your Muse. She's the guide behind stories that tug at your heartstrings and make you feel all sorts of emotions. She helps playwrights write about sadness and challenges, reminding us that even in tough times, stories can help us to understand the world.

Polyhymnia, The Muse of Sacred Poetry

Polyhymnia is the poet-priestess of the Muses. She inspires poets to write meaningful words that honour the gods and send blessings to people. Imagine her words as small prayers floating on the winds, carrying good wishes to those in need.

Terpsichore, The Muse of Dance

Meet Terpsichore, the dancing Muse. She's the one who makes dancers twirl, leap and spin like leaves caught in a playful breeze. When you watch a graceful ballet or energetic hip-hop, it's like her magic is bringing the stories to life through dance.

Thalia, The Muse of Comedy

Got a case of the giggles? Thalia's to blame! She's the funny one of the Muses, inspiring writers to write funny stories that make us laugh. Imagine her as a jokester, sprinkling chuckles and joy wherever she goes.

Urania, The Muse of Astronomy

Take a look out at the starry night. Well, say hello to Urania, the Muse of astronomy! She's a cosmic explorer, inspiring astronomers to study the mysteries of the vast universe. When you gaze up at the night sky, remember that her presence is there.

Think about what it would be like to have these Muses as your friends. Wouldn't that be wonderful? When you wanted to write poems, Calliope would whisper tales in your ear. When you wanted to be a musician, Euterpe could guide your fingers on the strings or voice to sing. Or maybe you wanted to study history, well Clio could share stories from the past with you. Together the Muses should inspire us all to explore our talents and then to share our ideas with the world. Go ahead, just like the ancient Greeks you too can be inspired by their magical powers!

CHAPTER 27
PERSEUS - THE SLAYER OF MEDUSA

Greetings, young heroes and adventurers! Prepare yourselves for we are about to dive into the epic tale of Perseus, a brave character who slayed the fearsome monster Medusa. Join us on this epic journey where we learn all about this hero, his quest and his legacy in Greek mythology. With brave courage and cunning wit, Perseus etched his name into the legends of history, inspiring countless generations to come.

Perseus was born to the mighty Zeus, King of the Gods, and the mortal princess Danaë. Blessed he was, however from the start his life was filled with danger! King Acrisius, his grandfather, was afraid of a prophecy saying that he would fall at the hands of Perseus. And so, to avoid this fate, he locked Danaë and Perseus in a chest which he threw into the sea. The chest crashed into the sea and washed ashore on the island of Seriphos where a kind fisherman rescued them. On the island Perseus grew up to be a strong and fearless young man. Yet he was unaware of his divine heritage.

Perseus' life was going well until one day it took a bad turn when the wicked King Polydectes plotted against him. Polydectes devised a sneaky plan. He set Perseus a seemingly impossible task, demanding that he bring him the head of the dreaded Gorgon, Medusa as a gift. Medusa was one of the three Gorgon sisters, with snakes for hair and a gaze that could turn anyone into stone. Many had dared to challenge her. And many had fallen or frozen in her stare. Armed with a magical sword from the gods and a polished shield, Perseus set out on his dangerous quest.

Hermes the messenger god and Athena the goddess of wisdom helped Perseus find the lair of Medusa. To avoid her deathly gaze he used his polished shield to look at Medusa's reflection instead of directly at her. Carefully he aimed his sword. With a swift strike, he cut off her head. But the quest was not over yet!

On his way back home, Perseus came across the beautiful princess Andromeda who was about to be sacrificed to a monster. Perseus couldn't bear to see an innocent girl suffer. With bravery he rescued her just in time using Medusa's petrifying head to freeze the monster. Andromeda's parents King Cepheus and Queen Cassiopeia were forever grateful. They welcomed Perseus into their family, he married Andromeda and they lived happily ever after.

Perseus's adventures and heroic feats contributed to him as a beloved figure in Greek mythology. He became a symbol of courage, cleverness, and determination. And he proved that even mortals could achieve greatness! His legacy continued through the generations, with many famous heroes and demigods tracing their ancestry back to him, including the great Heracles (Hercules). Forever more he became an inspiration for countless heroes and adventurers.

As we conclude our epic journey into the world of Perseus, the heroic slayer of Medusa, let us remember his courageous quests and his enduring legacy in Greek mythology. His stories teach us that bravery and determination can conquer even the most difficult of challenges. Along with the help of our friends and family we can overcome difficult challenges that might lay ahead.

So, young heroes, as you face your own adventures in life, remember Perseus. Let his bravery inspire you to be strong, smart and a great friend. May his legacy continue to inspire generations of brave souls like you. For even ordinary individuals like us can achieve amazing things!

CHAPTER 28

PRINCE THESEUS & HIS HEROIC ADVENTURES

Well hello there, young adventurers! Get ready to buckle up for a journey into the legendary tales of Theseus, the heroic Cretan Prince. Join us as we dive headfirst into his epic travels to claim his city of Athens. Are you ready to learn about his amazing adventures and his legacy as a leader of Athens? Well hurry up, the journey begins now!

Our story begins with the birth of Theseus, a prince like no other. His mother, Princess Aethra and his father, King Aegeus, had a unique plan. Under a massive rock, they laid a sword and sandals like a hidden treasure. Once Theseus could lift that rock to take those treasures, it would be his cue to travel to Athens and claim his royal destiny.

When the time was ready, Theseus headed out for the adventure of a lifetime. But hold on tight, because his journey was definitely not an easy one! Almost right away, he crossed paths with a gang of menacing thieves. Theseus wasn't one to back down in the face of these troublemakers' attempts to stop him. The brave prince faced them head-on. And what do you know? He triumphed! Theseus demonstrated that true bravery and quick thinking can overcome even the most brutal of bullies.

But that was just a small taste of his epic journeys! So young adventurers let us continue to unravel the tales of Theseus. Buckle up your seatbelts as our journey will be filled with twists, turns and triumph. Prepare to be inspired, to laugh, to gasp and to embark on an adventure you'll never forget!

Theseus's Famous Adventures

One of Theseus's most famous adventures was his encounter with the dreaded Minotaur. This fearsome creature with the head of a bull and the body of a man, was confined in a labyrinth below the island of Crete where King Minos ruled.

Every year the mean king demanded that Athens send human sacrifices to the Minotaur. Theseus was determined to put an end to this cruel tradition. When he arrived, Princess Ariadne, the daughter of King Minos, fell in love with him and helped him to slay the Minotaur. But we won't give you all the gory details here, for full details check out - CHAPTER 13: THE MAZE OF THE MINOTAUR!

Anyway, if you're still reading, this is what happened next! After successfully defeating the Minotaur, Theseus set sail for Athens with Princess Ariadne at his side. All that sailing was tiring and so they stopped for a snooze on the island of Naxos. Unfortunately, whilst Theseus was sleeping, the trickster god Dionysus lured Ariadne into his divine realm. Heartbroken, Theseus was left alone to continue his journey. Along the way encountered many more challenges, including battles with the fierce Amazons.

When he reached the city of Athens, Theseus became a wise and courageous leader. The story of his triumph over the Minotaur brought hope and inspiration to the people. He rose to fame as a beloved hero who stood for justice and power. Under his rule he united many regions and turned Athens into a great city.

As we near the end of our journey into the thrilling world of Theseus, the heroic Cretan Prince. Let us remember his courageous journey to Athens, his victory over the Minotaur and his inspiring leadership of Athens. Let us also remember his tragic love story with Ariadne. His stories teach us the importance of bravery, leadership and determination in the face of adversity. Even in the darkest of times, with the help of clever solutions and loyal friends, we can overcome the most challenging obstacles. Or when faced with mean bullies we can stand up for ourselves, be brave. So young adventurers let the story of Theseus inspire you to be courageous leaders and brave heroes in your own lives.

PART 4
MYTHS & LEGENDS

CHAPTER 29

PANDORA'S BOX - A CAUTIONARY TALE OF CURIOSITY

Greetings young seekers of knowledge and wisdom! In this chapter we're going to explore the curious tale of Pandora, the first woman created by the gods. Are you ready to learn about her infamous curiosity that led to the myth of "Pandora's box"? Great, because many valuable lessons can be found in this myth so please pay close attention!

Pandora was a very special creation for she was sculpted by the gods themselves. They took great care and craftsmanship with each deity providing their own gifts to her. Pandora was a true wonder, meant to be the most perfect creature to ever walk the earth. Hephaestus the blacksmith, gave her the gifts of beauty, intelligence and charm. Lastly, he also gave her one more very special gift. Stay tuned as we will soon discover the impact of one gift of particular interest, her insatiable curiosity.

Pandora's Box

Along with her many splendid gifts, the gods gave Pandora a mysterious box that was sealed tightly. But she was strictly instructed never to open it. Despite serious warnings from the gods, her curiosity grew and grew. The mystery inside the box was just too much to resist opening it. With her heart racing she slowly opened the lid, not knowing what to expect. As she opened the box to her shock and surprise, a whole swarm of troubles escaped out into the world! Pain, sickness, envy and all sorts of bad things spread out like a virus among humans causing sadness.

Pandora felt helpless, but, just when things seemed at their darkest she heard a faint whisper coming from inside the box. It was the last remaining spirit, hiding in there all along. Can you guess what it was? It was the spirit of hope! Even though Pandora had let lose lots of trouble into the world, she had also been given something precious, the gift of hope. Hope was still there like a glowing torch lighting up the night to guide people through even the darkest of times.

With the spirit of hope by her side, Pandora felt a surge of determination. She understood that while troubles and challenges were now a part of the world, hope was the key to overcoming them. The spirit of hope offered her a silent promise, that no matter how bad things got, there would always be a glimmer of light to guide others through the darkest of times.

Lessons from Pandora

The myth of Pandora's Box teaches us valuable lessons that are as old as time itself. You see, being curious is a natural part of being human...something that kids, like you, know very well! But just like crossing a busy street, we must be careful and follow the advice of those with more wisdom. Think of it like having a map when you're exploring a new place. We should always consider the consequences of our actions, just like a captain steering a ship through stormy seas. Stay curious because having an open mind is like a key that can open many doorways to endless discoveries. But remember, just like you'd wear a helmet while biking, always be careful and stay aware.

But wait, there's more to learn! Pandora also reminds us that life isn't always smooth sailing. Nope, sometimes we face challenges and difficulties that can feel like a bumpy roller coaster ride. But guess what? The power of hope can guide us even in the most difficult of times. Remember that even in the darkest of times, hope will always be there to guide you. Imagine hope as you're superhero friend who always has your back, that's the power of hope!

CHAPTER 30

THE TROJAN WAR - AN EPIC BATTLE OF HEROES, GODS & A WOODEN HORSE

Greetings, young warriors and history lovers! Prepare yourselves for tales from the epic Trojan War. In this chapter, we'll embark on an exciting journey to learn about the causes and key players of the Trojan War. But that's not all! We'll also discover the fascinating role of the gods and goddesses in the war. Then later we'll learn about the tragic aftermath of the war and its legacy in Greek mythology.

Now let's start at the beginning to discover what the Trojan War was all about. This legendary conflict took place between the ancient city of Troy and the mighty Greeks. The war was caused by a love affair between Prince Paris of Troy, and the beautiful Helen, wife of King Menelaus of Sparta. When Paris kidnapped Helen, Menelaus and his brother Agamemnon sent their armies to save her. The result was an epic war that captured the imagination of generations to come.

Many key characters and legends were involved in the Trojan War including brave heroes like Achilles, Hector, Odysseus, and Ajax leading the Greek forces. Valiant warriors such as Aeneas and Priam defended Troy. Meanwhile the gods and goddesses of Olympus also played key roles in the war. Battles were swayed by them as they took sides in the conflict, supporting either the Greeks or the Trojans.

Athena, the wise goddess, sided with the Greeks. She offered her guidance, strategy and protection to their heroes. Hera, the queen of the gods, also supported the Greeks, as did Poseidon, god of the sea, and Hermes, the messenger god. On the other side, Aphrodite, the goddess of love, favoured the Trojans. In fact, it was her involvement in the judgement of Paris, which started the whole affair. Apollo and Ares were among the gods and goddesses who supported the Trojans.

The Wooden Horse

After ten years of intense war the Greeks devised a sneaky

plan to finally get inside the highly guarded walls of Troy. Long battles had led to a stalemate and so they built a massive wooden horse. Inside it they hid their finest warriors to be sneaked in. Meanwhile the rest of the Greek army tricked the Trojans by pretending to retreat, leaving the wooden horse as a supposed peace offering.

The Trojans were tricked into a false sense of safety. Victory was in their hands they thought and moved the wooden horse into their city as a trophy. But little did they know that inside of it, Greek warriors were hidden! Inside the warriors waited for nightfall and under the cover of darkness they emerged from the wooden horse. They opened the city gates, allowing the rest of the Greek army to enter the city and in the chaos that followed Troy was defeated. A trail of sorrow and tragedy followed in the aftermath. Hector, the great Trojan hero, was killed by Achilles. Then more drama followed as Achilles was then slain by Paris to avenge the death of his brother. Finally the noble king of Troy was killed and the city was left in ruins.

The Trojan War became a legend in Greek mythology. Over many years, its stories have been retold and passed down through history. May you receive this timeless tale to fuel your own love for history and mythology! Valuable lessons of honour, courage and wisdom can be found in it. So, young warriors and history lovers, let the legend of the Trojan War inspire you to face challenges! For with honour, courage and wisdom you may overcome challenges. Let it guide you on your own epic adventures and quests for knowledge!

PART 5
EVEN MORE GODS & GODDESSES!

CHAPTER 31
THE TITANS & THEIR EPIC CLASH

Welcome brave young adventurers! Are you enjoying the journey so far? Well, it's great to have you here and in this magnificent chapter you're about to discover the Titans! Once upon a time these ancient and powerful gods ruled the cosmos in Greek mythology. In this chapter, we'll uncover their origins, significance in Greek Mythology and witness their epic clash, known as the Titanomachy!

Long, very long ago in fact before the reign of the Olympian gods, the Titans were born. Children of the heavens and earth, together they ruled over a vast and infinite universe. With immense power they embodied the elements of the earth, sky and sea. Each Titan possessed unique abilities that influenced the balance of the universe.

Clash of the Titans!

Picture this: an incredible showdown between the mighty Titans and their descendants, the Olympic Gods. Brace yourselves, for this legendary clash is known as the Titanomachy! It all began when Uranus, the first ruler of the Titans, was overthrown by his very own son, Cronus. Talk about a family feud! But Cronus, afraid of meeting the same fate as his father, had a rather strange solution...he would eat his own children as soon as they were born, yikes!

Cronus' wife Rhea couldn't bear to see her precious children gobbled up. So, she hatched a clever plan. When she gave birth to Zeus, she disguised him as a stone. Zeus grew up in secret, gaining strength and power. And guess what? He eventually became the ruler of all gods, the big boss up in Olympus!

But the story doesn't end there. Once Zeus was strong enough, he confronted his dad, Cronus, and released his siblings from their belly-imprisonment. It was like a family reunion of mythic proportions! And thus began the ultimate battle between the young and powerful Olympian gods and the Titans.

Can you imagine the cosmic clash that followed? Thunderbolts clashed, earth shook, and the sky rumbled as gods and Titans clashed for control of the universe. After a truly epic showdown the Olympian gods emerged victorious! They sent the Titans packing, banishing them deep into the shadows of Tartarus within the Underworld.

The Titans Legacy

As you gaze upon the stars and ponder the mysteries of the universe, remember the Titans and their legacy. Even in the world of gods and titans, the struggle for power and control is real. But with courage, determination, and maybe a bit of clever trickery, the underdogs – or in this case, the young Olympians – can rise to greatness. This myth reminds us that strength and unity can conquer even the mightiest challenges, making it a timeless tale of victory against all odds!

In the dance of the stars, galaxies and the mysteries of the universe together many questions are waiting to be explored. As you embark on your own journey of learning, approach it with an open mind and an eager heart. Just as the Titans dared to challenge the boundaries of the heavens, you too must challenge the limitations of your own understanding. Embrace change as the Titans did when they faced a new generation of gods, adapting in the face of adversity.

The universe, much like the Titans' struggle, is always moving and changing. With each passing discovery you are stepping into the realm of the unknown. Step forth with courage and determination young learners. For we must be willing to adapt to change, keep learning and stay hungry in our pursuit of knowledge.

CHAPTER 32
HADES - LORD OF THE UNDERWORLD

Greetings young explorers and brave adventurers! Are you ready to venture deep into the underworld? Prepare yourselves for some scary and enchanting tales within the realms of Hades, the powerful lord, God of the underworld. Don't worry we'll hold your hand as we uncover the scary but fascinating Hades! Welcome to his domain, the underworld, the afterlife and the Eleusinian Mysteries.

Hades was the brother of Zeus and Poseidon. As the mighty lord, God of the underworld he was responsible for judging souls that entered into his realm. He reigned over the underworld, a place that was hidden, deep beneath the earth. It was here in this kingdom that the spirits of the deceased travelled to after they had left the mortal world. Imagine such a mysterious and eerie place where the afterlife lived on! But it wasn't all doom and gloom...as we'll soon discover.

Actually, there was more to it than meets the eye. While "Tartarus" was a place of punishment for the wicked, the "Fields of Asphodel" were a neutral and peaceful place for ordinary souls. And of course, there were the "Isles of the Blessed" which were a paradise for heroes and virtuous souls.

Within the underworld was The River Styx, another fascinating place. It was a boundary between the mortal world and the underworld. Those souls who came to the underworld first had to cross the Styx in the boat of Charon who would only accept payment in one way. One had to place a coin under the tongue of the dead!

The Elysian Mysteries

In the heart of the Underworld was a place of eternal beauty known as Elysium. Heroes and anyone who had lived honourable lives were granted a special afterlife here. The Elysian Mysteries were not just about the physical wonders of Elysium but also about its magical secrets and rituals.

Mysteries that unlocked the hidden treasures of the Underworld, allowing only those who were worthy to experience its true magic.

But how did one join the Elysian Mysteries? Well, it wasn't as simple as raising your hand and saying, "I want to join!" No, the process was a bit more mystical. It involved special rituals, ceremonies, and tests to prove one's worthiness.

The Elysian Mysteries were a celebration of life and its potential for greatness. They encouraged people to strive for goodness, to be kind to others, and to embrace their inner hero. And just as heroes were welcomed into Elysium, those who celebrated the mysteries were also welcomed into the special community.

The Story of Hades and Persephone

The tale of Hades and Persephone is one of the most magical love stories in Greek mythology. One day, as Hades was roaming the fields of the human world when he came across the radiant Persephone. She was the daughter of Demeter, the Goddess of Agriculture. Her beauty mesmerised and captivated Hades. He was so obsessed and just had to make her his Queen of the underworld.

Hades hatched his cunning plan and on one, fateful day as Persephone was picking flowers he appeared before her in a chariot drawn by majestic, black horses. He swept her away to his kingdom, but this caused great distress to her mother Demeter. Persephone also felt lonely and homesick in the underworld. She yearned to return to the world of living. Hades insisted on making her his queen and tricked her into eating some pomegranate seeds. Such a trick unknowingly sealed her fate to spend part of every year in the end of the world. From then on Persephone would have to spend six months of every year with Hades in the underworld. Without her radiant beauty the earth became cold and experienced harsh winters during. When she returned to her mother Demeter, the world would bloom with joy and beauty.

Now as we conclude our own journey...but not one into the underworld but rather one onwards in our own lives let us remember the cautious tales of Hades. Seek the truth, young friend. Understand that many times we will explore further the stories or rumours to find out what the truth is. Because sometimes what is talked about as being bad may have something good going on behind the scenes. Just like the underworld and its hidden paradises. Remember there are dark and light sides to everything. When we seek the truth that we are moving more towards the light. Remember that all of your actions have consequences, and if you practise honesty then you will live a virtuous life.

CHAPTER 33
THE FATES - WEAVERS OF DESTINY

Once upon a time, long, long ago in the magical world of ancient Greece there lived three special sisters with powers to shape the future. Togethery they were known as the fates and together they guided the lives of everyone in the world. Each had their own unique role in the process of creating destiny. The future of mortals, gods and even you would be influenced by them! Are you ready to look into the future? Brave you are indeed! Now let's learn more about these mysterious women.

Clotho: The Spinner of Life

Clotho was the youngest of the three sisters and hers was a very important job. She was known as the spinner of life. Imagine her sitting by a giant spinning wheel where she would spin the threads of people's lives. With every twist and turn of her wheel, she threaded out a new life journey. Thankfully she was kind and generous, making sure that everyone had a fair chance.

Lachesis: The Measurer of Fate

Lachesis was the middle sister. She was the measurer of fate and her role required great care. With her magical measuring stick, she measured the threads spun by Clotho. With the thread in her hands, she calculated how long each person's journey would be. It might be a quick trip or it might be a lengthy one. Who knows? Lachesis did. She knew exactly how long each person needed to experience the world.

Atropos: The Cutter of Threads

Atropos was the eldest sister and her task was the most mysterious. Once Lachesis measured the thread, Atropos would decide when it was time for it to end. With her sharp scissors, she would carefully cut the thread to signal the end of a person's life. Now this might sound sad, but Atropos knew that every ending was also the beginning of something new. It all depended on how one viewed it.

Together the three fates worked, weaving the tapestry of life for everyone in the world. Imagine them as masterful artists creating fantastic patterns. Patterns that told the lives of heroes, kings, queens, gods and even ordinary people like us. No two threads were the same and every person's thread was unique. The fates made sure life was full of surprises, challenges and opportunities along the way.

Young scholars as you journey through life remember the fates and their magical work. Let them remind you that life is a beautiful tapestry woven with love, laughter, challenges and adventures. Make the most of every moment and cherish the time that you have on this earth. Stay present and grateful. Just like the fates we have the power to shape our own destinies by the choices that we make. Regardless of where we are from or the cards we were dealt, it is in our hands. Venture forth with a smile and let your unique thread of life lead you on a wonderful journey!

CHAPTER 34
PROMETHEUS –
THE GIFT GIVER

Good day young adventurers! Are you ready to begin a thrilling new quest? Join us as we journey into the extraordinary tales of Prometheus. This heroic Titan gifted humanity with a wonderful treasure, fire! Here in this chapter, we'll first discover the creation of humans and how Prometheus was involved in the process. Finally, we'll learn about how he stole fire from the gods to help humanity and the cruel punishment he received. Let's go!

In the olden days, the gods of Mount Olympus ruled from above the heavens whilst the mighty Titans ruled the earth. After taking in the wonders of the world, the Olympians decided to create something new. Something was missing in the world below, what was it they wondered? Humans! Prometheus, a Titan, was given the responsibility of creating humans by Zeus the ruler of the gods.

Prometheus was famous for his intelligence, making him the perfect guardian of humanity. He took great care in creating humans, giving them various gifts and abilities. He taught them how to build homes, farm the lands, and how to work with tools and weapons. Finally, he gave them the gifts of power, intelligence, curiosity and taught them all about the world around them.

Prometheus Steals Fire from the Gods

In the realms of Mount Olympus fire was a sacred treasure that was possessed only by the gods. It brought light and warmth, but more importantly it symbolised knowledge and civilization. These were the very elements that could help humanity to reach new heights. Prometheus saw the potential of fire to help his human creations. However, he would first have to steal it from the gods. As you can imagine this would be a daring and dangerous task.

Now, let's set the scene. Picture Mount Olympus, the grand

home of the mighty gods. One fateful night, as the gods peacefully slept, Prometheus tiptoed into their divine home. His heart pounded like drum beats when he saw the fire of the gods. With courage he silently approached, his palms sweaty with anticipation. Gently, as though cradling a star in his hands, he captured a single glowing ember from the flames. Oh, the excitement! It sent shivers down his spine.

And so, with the radiant gift of fire tucked safely into his possession, Prometheus began his descent from the heavenly realm. The air around him crackled with energy and the stars above twinkled. As he journeyed back to the world of mortals, held within his hands was a treasure that would forever change humanity. The gift lighted up their lives, providing warmth against the cold and providing light in the darkness.

But wait! Zeus, the all-seeing ruler of the gods, soon found out about Prometheus's tricky act. And he was furious! Angrily he chained him to a mountainside where an eagle would feast on his liver everyday. What a horrible fate! But this punishment did not break his spirit. Even though he was in a lot of pain, he would not plead with Zeus. In the end, he knew that any suffering was worth giving the humans the gift of fire.

Prometheus became more than a hero. For the humans he was their light on a pathway through dark times. Through the ages his very name was whispered like a secret promise of empowerment. Indeed, his heroic efforts came at a great personal cost, that locked him in chains. But despite his suffering, his spirit remained unconquerable, thus demonstrating the power of the human spirit.

As you read the tales of Prometheus, let his dedication remind you that even in the face of challenges, you have the power to spark change. Just as Prometheus lit the fire for humans, your own efforts can ignite a flame of positive change for others. And as you venture through life let your light shine brightly like a raging fire!

CHAPTER 35
EROS (CUPID) - THE MISCHIEVOUS GOD OF LOVE

Ah, love is in the air, young hearts! In this dear chapter we're about to learn about Eros, the mischievous and delightful god of love. Prepare to be carried away on the wings of this god in adventure where we'll learn all about him and the magical effect of his love arrows. Now let us dive into the depths of Greek mythology to explore love and passion in the enchanting world of Eros. Are you ready to embark?

High up on Mount Olympus where the gods and goddesses lived, Eros reigned as the god of love. Ever heard the name Cupid? Well, that was also his name and he was the son of Aphrodite, goddess of love, beauty and desire. We're sure you've seen him before. He's the winged, playful god with a magical bow and arrows in his hands. But these are no ordinary arrows...they're love arrows! With one strike they had the power to make mortals or even gods fall in love with whomever the arrow might strike.

In Greek mythology, Eros was not only a symbol of romantic love. He was much more. Imagine the gentle affection shared between parents and children. Eros's touch can be felt in the laughter exchanged between siblings, the soothing embrace of a mother's arms and the protective watch of a father's gaze. Think of your dearest friends, those kindred spirits who light up your world with their presence. With his arrows of affection, he weaves strong bonds of friendship.

Eros' Mischievous Adventures

With his bow and love arrows in hand, Eros went on many great adventures, stirring up emotions of the gods and mortals alike. He loved to matchmake and find couples to fall in love with each other. Whenever he fired his arrows, couples would fall head over heels for each other. Often it led to happy, romantic and heartfelt connections. Even the mighty gods and goddesses could not resist Eros' love arrows! Amazingly some of the gods and goddesses even fell in love with humans. Of course, this led to some dramatic love stories!

In Greek mythology Eros represents the force of love that binds humans together which inspires affection, compassion and devotion. With his love arrows he sparks the flames of passion leading to both joyous, and sometimes dramatic affairs.

Tales of Eros remind us of love's powerful force that can bring joy, healing and unity. Love goes beyond couples. There is also love between friends, family and the world around us. Indeed, it has the potential of heartache but grief is a price worthy of paying for love. For love is an important part of being human. Maybe the most important part.

As we conclude this loving chapter let us remember the magic of Eros and his tales of love and adventure. Let it all remind you of the importance of love in our lives. Love your friends and family with warmth. Share your love with the world. For love is a wondrous force and we should cherish those precious moments together with our loved ones. Be kind to the world around you and love all of its creatures. May the spirit of Eros' love always dance within your hearts!

PART 6
GREEK CULTURE & LEGACY

CHAPTER 36
ANCIENT GREEK HEROES IN THE MODERN WORLD

Greetings young scholars of Greek mythology. Welcome to the beginning of a new journey into exploring how ancient Greek myths and heroes have continued to influence us today. From books to movies and to artwork we're about to delve into some of the famous retellings and adaptations of Greek myths in popular culture. Many years later in this present day you'll discover why they still captivate audiences. In addition, we'll also discover examples of Greek mythology in our everyday language. Are you ready to discover the timeless wonders of Greek mythology? Well then let's begin.

Ahh Greek Mythology, its allure is mesmerising and it continues to be found in modern culture. Writers, filmmakers and artists from around the world continue to draw inspiration from the epic tales of ancient Greece. In books many famous authors have created compelling stories that were inspired by Greek myths whose heroes set out on epic quests to overcome challenges and dilemmas. Themes of bravery, sacrifice, and the struggle between good and evil are still popular to this day because they carry universal messages. Naturally this makes them relatable to readers of diverse backgrounds.

The magic of Greek mythology has also found its way into the cinema. Directors and screenwriters continue to be inspired by classic myths in blockbuster movies. We've seen on screen the myths of Perseus, Hercules and Medusa. All of these and many more have been reimagined and recreated in a number of different variations on the silver screen. Filling a spectrum of emotions and thrilling tales.

In the world of fine art ancient Greek influences can still be found to this day. From the majestic statues of Greek gods and goddesses found in public places to the paintings of mythological scenes. The vibrant legacy of ancient Greece continues to inspire artists to create masterpieces around the world.

Famous Retellings and Adaptations of Greek Myths

Rick Riordan's "Percy Jackson & the Olympians" series, brings Greek gods and heroes into the modern world. Readers can escape into the thrilling adventures and humorous escapades.

The film "Troy" explores the legendary Trojan War, showcasing the valour of Achilles and the struggles of Hector. New audiences can enjoy the epic saga once again.

"Wonder Woman," the beloved superheroine, draws inspiration from the Amazonian warrior princess. Again the epics of Greek mythology are found in modern storytelling.

Greek Mythology in Modern Language

Greek mythology has even found its way into our everyday modern language.

Phrases like "Achilles' heel" to refer to a weak point.

Whilst "Pandora's box" relates to something that might create unwanted consequences.

Then there is the saying of a "Herculean task". One would imagine a tremendous challenge in this case!

Even some of the stars in the night sky are named after characters from Greek myths. The constellation Orion is named after the great hunter Orion. Whilst the Pleiades, constellation is named after the seven daughters of the Titan Atlas.

We can all find some similarities in Greek mythology because ultimately, they connect with the experience of being human. These ancient tales resonate with our emotions, dreams and struggles. They capture our dilemmas and troubles which are timeless and universal. Struggles of heroes reflect courage and echo through the ages. Whilst moral dilemmas of the gods send important messages across generations.

Truly these stories are timeless and will live on forever in our world. Forever they will connect us to the amazing experience of being human which spans cultures, centuries and transcends language. Timeless tales touch the heart and ignite our imagination. Indeed, we can all relate them to our own struggles, triumphs and dreams.

Since the beginning of time humanity has pursued greatness. We have sought love and friendship. At the same time, we fight an eternal struggle between light and darkness. May the legacy of Greek Mythology inspire you on your own journeys and heroic quests! For many, many years (since before you were born) these myths have captivated the minds of the world. And for many more years they will!

CHAPTER 37

THE GREEK OLYMPICS - HONOURING THE GODS THROUGH SPORTS

Get ready to step into the thrilling world of the ancient Greek olympics! An event of the strongest, fastest and fittest. Here athletes gathered to showcase their skills in honour of the mighty gods and goddesses of Mount Olympus. Within this chapter we'll journey back in time to uncover the origins of the Greek olympics which have lasted until this day. As we uncover this grand sporting event let us also explore its connection to Greek religion and mythology. Get ready, it's time to stretch your muscles and tie up your shoelaces!

We begin our journey back to 776 BC in the city state of Olympia. It was at this moment that the ancient Greek Olympics began in honour of Zeus the king of gods. Greeks from various cities united in this event of competition and camaraderie. Held every four years, these games soon became a celebrated tradition.

The Olympics were of great importance both culturally and religiously for the Greeks. Athletes had the opportunity to show off their physical skills. But more than that it represented the harmony between the human world and the heavens above. Winners in the games were celebrated as heroic athletes and the favourites of the gods. Their victories were believed to be the results of God's blessings.

Olympic Sports

The Greek Olympics included many different sports and competitions. Each with their own demanding skills and abilities. Among some of the most popular events were:

Running races

The stadium where the Greek Olympics were held featured a track for short sprints and long running races. Speed and endurance would be demonstrated by the finest runners of those times.

Wrestling

Two athletes would face each other in this intense sport. Whoved submitted their opponent to the ground would emerge victorious.

Discus Throw

Strong athletes would throw a heavy discus (kind of like a heavy frisbee) as far as possible. Whoever could throw the discus furthest would emerge victorious.

Javelin Throw

Mighty athletes would throw a javelin (kind of like a spear) as far as possible. Whoever landed the furthest was the winner.

Chariot Racing

This thrilling sport involved skilled horse riders guiding a chariot connected to the horse in an epic race to the finish line.

Pankration

This was a fierce combination of boxing and wrestling (kind of like mixed martial arts) where athletes had to use all of their skills and powers to emerge victorious.

How the Olympics Connected to Greek Religion and Culture

For the ancient Greeks the Olympics were more than just a sporting event. It was also a sacred occasion celebrating religious beliefs to further connect them to the gods. Before every Olympic event, athletes and spectators would join in elaborate ceremonies where they would make offerings to the gods seeking their favour.

What's amazing is that many Greek city states were sometimes involved in battle but during the Olympic Games they would pause the war in a truce! This was known as the

"Olympic Peace,". During this time all wars were suspended. All athletes and fans could now travel safely to and from Olympia without fear of harm. The Olympic Peace was a symbol of unity and demonstrated the shared values of Greek culture. Truly sports and competition has the power to heal.

To this day the Olympics live on as a worldwide event. They are testament to the unity between people and the respect between cultures. Regardless of our differences we can set them aside to celebrate healthy competition and to inspire each other.

Well young athletes as we come to the end of this brilliant chapter let us celebrate the Greek Olympics. Such a magnificent event that honours the gods through sports uniting together people from all corners of ancient Greece. As you run, jump and play, may you remember the spirit of the Greek Olympics. Embrace the spirit of sportsmanship, respect and honour. Let it fuel your own journey to greatness. Until our next adventure may the gods and goddesses blessings be with you on your journey to becoming true champions!

CHAPTER 38
GREEK HEROES IN EVERYDAY LIFE

Listen closely to young readers because we're about to uncover some hidden lessons from ancient Greek Heroes that will help us in our daily lives. Pay close attention as we dive deep into the virtues and characters of these legendary figures. With the lessons learned it will help to shine a light on our own pathways. Maybe you can also become heroes in the world!

The great heroes of ancient Greece were more than just mighty warriors; they were also wise and virtuous characters. And their stories teach us valuable life lessons that we can apply in our own lives. Let's learn!

Courage

From the fearless Perseus who faced the scary monster Medusa to the brave Hercules who conquered the Twelve Labors. Greek heroes inspired bravery in the face of tough times. Courage doesn't mean that you won't feel afraid. But it is your ability to rise above fear even when you feel it.

Compassion

Heroes like Theseus and Jason showed compassion and empathy towards others. Together with their friends and fellow warriors they achieved great things. Learn from their kindness and compassion. Whatever you want from the world you should learn to give it first, because in giving we can find true strength.

Wisdom

Athena the great goddess of wisdom guided many heroes with her intelligent advice. Wise decisions come from learning and experience. We should seek wisdom from our elders and continue to learn. Thus, we should also learn from our own experiences. Such wisdom will help us to make better decisions in our life.

Perseverance

Do you remember Odysseus' epic journey home? And do you remember Persephone's determination to rescue her kidnapped daughter? These stories and many more from Greek mythology showcase the power of perseverance. Young friends, never give up on your dreams! All too often we stop short when we are very close to achieving our goals. Master perseverance to unlock the doors of your success.

Modern Heroes

Heroes don't just exist in Greek mythology; they also exist in the world around us. Everyday there are heroes who risk their lives for others. Firefighters, police officers, volunteers and first responders are just a few of the many heroes in our modern world. Selfishly they dedicate their time and effort to support those in need. Be inspired by them and consider the ways that you too can help in this modern world.

Remember young readers that being a hero is not only about grand gestures or epic events. Sometimes small acts of kindness and compassion can make a huge difference in the lives of others. For you too young readers have the power to be a hero in your own community and make a positive impact on the world around you. Simple acts of kindness such as helping a friend in need or showing empathy to someone going through a tough time can make a huge difference.

Don't let bullies or injustice continue. Stand up against evil. Get involved in your community, serve others, volunteer and make a positive contribution. You can also be a role model by embodying the virtues of Greek Heroes to inspire others by being your very best self.

As we conclude our journey in this empowering chapter let us again remember that heroism is not just for the extraordinary. Each and every one of us has the power to be a hero in small or big ways. Embrace the virtues of the Greek Myths and let them serve you as guiding stars towards a life of courage and compassion. Never underestimate the power of your actions, young readers, even the smallest acts of kindness can create ripples of positive change. Embrace the hero within yourself. Now more than ever the world needs heroes like you and together we can create a better future.

CONCLUSION

Congratulations young explorers you have reached the grand finale of a thrilling journey through the world of Greek gods, goddesses, heroes and monsters! As we conclude this epic adventure let us remember the legacy of Greek mythology and refresh the valuable lessons from these timeless myths.

Just like the great majestic phoenix rises from the ashes, Greek mythology has continued to stand the test of time. For countless generations its magical tales have continued to captivate imaginations and spark inspiration in hearts. Stories of brave heroes, powerful gods and mythical creatures have lasted for centuries. From the courage and determination of heroes like Hercules and Perseus. To the wisdom and strategic thinking of Athena. Each myth, God, goddess, hero and even the monsters convey important lessons to learn.

Virtues of courage, friendship and empathy can be found countless times in Greek mythology. Through triumph and tragedy these larger than life stories and characters have taught us the importance of friendship, honour and perseverance. Lessons found inside also taught us the consequences of wrongdoing, jealousy and greed. Cautionary tales like these will help us to guide us to better life choices.

Over the centuries authors, play rights and poets have drawn inspiration from the epic tales of the ancient Greek. Mythological elements have been weaved into their masterpieces to enchant and captivate readers. Whilst filmmakers and animators have brought gods, heroes, monsters and mythology to life on the movie screen. Artists too have been inspired; sculpting magnificent statues and crafting inspiring paintings to celebrate the immortal beauty of Greek mythology.

Now today, the magical world of Greek mythology awaits

you forevermore! You have a duty to pass these tales down to the next generation. Share them as you embark on your own quest of discovery and continue to learn from these ancient myths. For within them remain infinite opportunities for learning, growth and enlightenment. We encourage you to keep learning and to re-read or re-listen this book because each time new insights will appear related to your current situation.

May your imagination soar high like Icarus and your determination be as strong as Odysseus on his journey home. Let your spirit fly on the wings of Perseus, dive into the deep ocean with Poseidon and solve riddles with the wise Sphinx! Stand brave and strong like Hercules, wise like Athena and kind like Persphone.

As we say goodbye to the world of Greek mythology, we hope you leave your hearts filled with wonder and a mind eager for more adventures. Of course, we will be back soon! Remember young learners that the legacy of Greek mythology can live on through you and every generation that follows. Take on the lessons and values from these ancient tales and share them with the world. You can make a positive change.

And as we close this journey, we leave you with one final thought:

You are the authors of your own destiny, the creators of your own myths and the heroes of your own stories.

Let the spirit of Greek mythology inspire you to dream big, dare greatly and to make a positive impact on the world. Until the next time we meet (coming soon), goodbye young adventurers! May the legacy of Greek mythology forever inspire wonder, strength and wisdom within you!

ACTIVITIES

ACTIVITY INFORMATION

Congratulations, young mythologists! As you conclude your journey through the captivating world of Greek gods, goddesses, and heroes, we have some exciting activities for you. These will help you to explore further and immerse yourself in the enchanting realm of Greek mythology. Not only will these activities entertain you but they will also deepen your understanding and connection with the mythical tales.

So, let's dive right in!

ACTIVITY 1
MYTHOLOGICAL RIDDLES

Welcome to the world of Ancient Greek Riddles!

Are you ready to challenge your knowledge and thinking skills? Prepare yourselves for we are about to present you with some complicated riddles. Now pay close attention to the descriptions and hints which are coming up.

Listen or read closely to the following riddles about some mythological characters. Don't rush, carefully think about the clues and hints found within the riddles. Take a guess at answering the riddles. Ask your friends and family for help. Then once you've made your guess go ahead to the reveal part to discover if you were correct.

Riddle 1

I am mighty and wise, a queen of all gods,

My husband is Zeus, the ruler of skies,

Far and wide my jealous nature cries,

But beware of my wrathe for it's not easy to hide.

Who am I?

Riddle 2

I rule the seas with my trident in hand,

Stormy waves are under my command,

Dolphins and horses they understand,

The depths of the oceans follow my demand.

Who am I?

Riddle 3

I was born from the head of Zeus, wise and fair,

Athens is the city for which I care,

My shield and helmet are symbols so grand,

In peace and war I lend my helping hand.

Who am I?

Riddle 4

Under the darkness i dwell and rule the dead,

The underworld is my home and it is widespread,

My queen Persephone is by my side,

The underworld's secrets here we hide.

Who am I?

Riddle 5

With my wings I fly quicker than a bee,

My messages of gods are the key,

With grace I guide souls, my role profound,

In the underworld my cleverness is renowned.

Who am I?

Riddle 6

With bow and arrows I'm a mischievous lad,

But in matters of love my aim is not bad,

When hearts flutter and emotions ignite,

With a strike of my arrow love burns bright.

Who am I?

Riddle 7

A monster feared with one gaze you will be stone,

With snakes for her she stands alone,

This gorgon is so grim to put you at unease,

One sight of her will make you freeze.

Who am I?

Riddle 8

A strong hero, his legend spreads wide,

Twelve labours he completed with pride,

With the strength of gods in his heart,

And with bare hands he tore beasts apart.

Who am I?

Riddle 9

I am poet who plays a music divine,

With my melodies stands still time,

I went to the underworld to win back love,

And played beautiful songs, gentle as a dove.

Who am I?

Riddle 10

Inside a box lay many mysteries untold,

Be warned if you open it trouble might unfold,

One fair maiden opened it at a cost,

Despair unfolded but hope was not lost.

Who am I?

Dear readers behold the ten riddles! Do you know the answers? Seek wisdom from your friends and family. Now write down your answers and check at the end. If you were successful then celebrate, otherwise study more young friends!

ACTIVITY 2
THE MYTHOLOGY QUIZ SHOW

Greetings and welcome to the mythology quiz show! Your expert mythology skills are about to be tested. Are you ready for the challenge? Listen or read carefully because you are about to be presented with a quiz about many things which you have learned in this book.

You can join with family, friends or alone. But one rule must be followed...don't skip ahead to the answers! For each question you will be given multiple options. Wise young scholars think carefully before choosing your answer. If you're not sure, use your best instincts or ask for advice. Write down all of your answers and when you're finished check the correct answers at the end of this book. Good luck!

Question 1

Who was the king that ruled the gods and goddesses of Mount Olympus?

a) Hera
b) Poseidon
c) Zeus
d) Apollo

Question 2

Which goddess was famous for wisdom and strategy in war?

a) Aphrodite
b) Athena
c) Artemis
d) Hestia

Question 3

Which god ruled the sea, holding a powerful trident?

a) Hades
b) Apollo
c) Poseidon
d) Hermes

Question 4

What was the name of the hero that completed twelve labours?

a) Perseus
b) Theseus
c) Heracles (Hercules)
d) Odysseus

Question 5

What was the name of the goddess of love, beauty and desire?

a) Hera
b) Artemis
c) Demeter
d) Aphrodite

Question 6

What was the name of the god of the messenger of the gods?

a) Hermes
b) Dionysus
c) Ares
d) Hephaestus

Question 7

Who was the goddess connected with the changing seasons?

a) Hera
b) Demeter
c) Athena
d) Hestia

Question 8

Who was the wife of Hades, God of the underworld?

a) Persephone
b) Artemis
c) Athena
d) Aphrodite

Question 9

Which mythical beasts had the head of a human and the body of a lion?

a) Centaur
b) Minotaur
c) Sphinx
d) Chimera

Question 10

Which hero went to the underworld to rescue his lover?

a) Orpheus
b) Jason
c) Theseus
d) Odysseus

Now young mythologists, prepare your answers. It's time to find out how much you truly know! Choose your best answers and check them at the end of this book. Keep a track of your results and continue to learn more about Greek mythology.

ACTIVITY 3
MYTHICAL COOKING

Well, hello there! Are you feeling hungry? All of this learning has for sure will have burned some calories and fueled appetites. Get ready for a feast! We are about to discover some fun and delicious recipes inspired by Greek mythology.

Listen or read carefully these recipes. Make sure you have an adult to help you gather everything you need. Follow the steps to create these mythical dishes. Then when they're ready, enjoy eating them with your friends and families. Now young chefs let's get to the cooking!

Recipe 1: Ambrosia Fruit Salad

Here we go! We are about to discover a divine dish for the gods themselves, Ambrosia Fruit Salad! Ask an adult and let's gather all of the ingredients to create this mythical treat.

Ingredients

- 1 cup of chopped pineapple
- 1 cup of orange cut up
- 1 cup of shredded coconut
- 1 cup of marshmallows
- 1 cup of seedless grapes
- 1 cup of Greek yoghurt
- 1 tablespoon of honey (optional, for a touch of sweetness)
- A handful of cherries (optional)

Instructions

Combine the chopped pineapple, orange cut up, shredded coconut, marshmallows, and seedless grapes. In another bowl mix the Greek yogurt with the optional honey for a creamy and sweet dressing. Pour the creamy dressing over the fruits and gently mix them until all the ingredients are covered.

Put the bowl in the fridge with some plastic wrap to cover it. Leave it there to meld for about thirty minutes. Next you can add some cherries for an extra touch of mythical charm.

Now it's time to enjoy this ambrosial delight! Savour the heavenly taste worthy of the gods and goddesses with your family and friends.

Recipe 2: Hercules' Hero Sandwiches

Hercules was a strong and powerful hero. So of course, he always needed big and hearty meals to fuel his muscles and adventures! The Hercules' Hero Sandwiches is such a hearty meal worthy of this hero.

Now with adult supervision, gather your ingredients and kitchen tools. Let's make these legendary sandwiches.

Ingredients

- 4 slices of buttered bread
- 8 slices of ham or turkey
- 8 slices of cooked bacon
- 4 slices of cheese
- Lettuce leaves
- Sliced tomatoes
- Sliced red onions
- Pickles (optional)
- Mayonnaise or mustard, for spreading

Instructions

Lay out the slices of bread on a clean surface. Spread butter on them. Next spread mayonnaise and mustard on one side of each piece of bread. Layer the ham or turkey, cooked bacon, and cheese on one piece bread. On the next piece of bread add the lettuce leaves, sliced tomatoes, red onions, and pickles. Press the bread slices lightly together and secure them with toothpicks if needed.

Now it's time for you to serve Hercules' Hero Sandwiches with a side of ambrosia fruit salad for a truly mythical feast! Enjoy your epic sandwiches and feel the strength and courage of Hercules as you take each heroic bite!

Young mythologists, savour the flavours of these mythical dishes and share them with your loved ones. May these recipes inspire you to create your own recipes and continue your journey into the enchanting world of Greek mythology!

ACTIVITY ANSWERS

<u>Warning, warning! Don't come here before you have completed the activities!!</u>

Activity One Answers:

Riddle 1: Hera

Riddle 2: Poseidon

Riddle 3: Athena

Riddle 4: Hades

Riddle 5: Hermes

Riddle 6: Eros (Cupid)

Riddle 7: Medusa

Riddle 8: Hercules

Riddle 9: Orpheus

Riddle 10: Pandora

Activity Two Answers:

Question 1

Who was the king that ruled the gods and goddesses of Mount Olympus?

c) Zeus

Question 2

Which goddess was famous for wisdom and strategy in war?

b) Athena

Question 3

Which God ruled the sea, holding a powerful trident?

c) Poseidon

Question 4

What was the name of the hero that completed twelve labours?

c) Heracles (Hercules)

Question 5

What was the name of the goddess of love, beauty and desire?

d) Aphrodite

Question 6

What was the name of the god of the messenger of the gods?

a) Hermes

Question 7

Who was the goddess connected with the changing seasons?

b) Demeter

Question 8

Who was the wife of Hades, God of the underworld?

a) Persephone

Question 9

Which mythical beasts had the head of a human and the body of a lion?

c) Sphinx

Question 10

Which hero went to the underworld to rescue his lover?

a) Orpheus

REFERENCES

PRIMARY REFERENCES

- This book is intended for informational and entertainment purposes only. Readers should not rely solely on its content for making important decisions or drawing conclusions. If you have concerns about the accuracy of any information presented in this book, please seek additional sources and expert advice.

- OpenAI. (2023). ChatGPT 3.5 https://chat.openai.com
This book was written with the assistance of ChatGPT, a language model developed by OpenAI, which provided creative input based on the information and instructions provided. While ChatGPT was used to aid in the writing process, the publishers of this book have made every effort to ensure the accuracy of the information presented. Extensive fact-checking and research were conducted to verify the information contained within this book.

- Mid Journey. (2023). https://www.midjourney.com/
All interior images were created with the use of artificial intelligence, namely Mid Journey.

OTHER BOOKS BY
HISTORY BROUGHT ALIVE

Available now in Ebook, Paperback, Hardcover, and
Audiobook in all regions.

For Kids:

GREEK LEGENDS FOR KIDS

We sincerely hope you enjoyed our new book *"Greek Legends for Kids"*. We would greatly appreciate your feedback with an honest review at the place of purchase.

First and foremost, we are always looking to grow and improve as a team. It is reassuring to hear what works, as well as receive constructive feedback on what should improve. Second, starting out as an unknown author is exceedingly difficult, and Amazon reviews go a long way toward making the journey out of anonymity possible. Please take a few minutes to write an honest review.

Best regards,
History Brought Alive
http://historybroughtalive.com/